GCE AS Level Single Award

D1081431

AS Level for OCR

Travel &
Tourism

Hilary Blackman • John D. Smith • Ann Rowe

Heinemann

Inspiring generations

Heinemann Educational Publishers
Halley Court, Jordan Hill, Oxford OX2 8EJ
Part of Harcourt Education

Heinemann is the registered trademark of
Harcourt Education Limited

© Hilary Blackman, Ann Rowe, John Smith, 2005

First published 2005

10 09 08 07 06 05
10 9 8 7 6 5 4 3 2 1

British Library Cataloguing in Publication Data is available
from the British Library on request.

ISBN 0 435 44640 1

20 64001 284

Designed by Lorraine Inglis
Typeset by 🗚 Tek-Art, Croydon, Surrey
Original illustrations © Harcourt Education Limited, 2005

Cover design by Wooden Ark Studio
Printed by Printer Trento Srl
Cover photo: © Alamy
Picture research by Bea Thomas

Acknowledgements
Every effort has been made to contact copyright holders of material
reproduced in this book. Any omissions will be rectified in
subsequent printings if notice is given to the publishers.

Websites
Please note that the examples of websites suggested in this book were
up to date at the time of writing. It is essential for tutors to preview
each site before using it to ensure that the URL is still accurate and
the content is appropriate. We suggest that tutors bookmark useful
sites and consider enabling student to access them through the school
or college intranet.

Tel: 01865 888058 www.heinemann.co.uk

Contents

Acknowledgements

The authors and publisher would like to thank all who have given permission to reproduce material.

Aston Business School, Aston University – page 85
Barcelona City Council Tourist Information, www.bcn.es – pages 111–12
Billing Aquadrome – page 7
Blencathra Field Centre, the Field Studies Council, www.field-studies-council.org – pages 117–9
Cambridge University Press – page 77
Columbus Travel – page 97
Co-op Travelcare – page 25
Cresta Holidays Ltd – page 85
Daily Mail – page 63
Diggerland – page 30
Falcon's Nest Hotel – page 44
Fast Track 100 Ltd – page 26
Government of Dubai Department of Tourism and Commerce Marketing – page 103, 107
Great North Eastern Railway (GNER) – page 80
Holiday Inn – page 33
Isle of Man Government – page 49
Isle of Man Transport – page 48
Lily Publications – pages 41, 45, 47
Manchester Airport Group plc – pages 89–90
Manx National Heritage – pages 42–3
National Trust – pages 28, 61
Northampton Borough Council – page 27
Norwich Area Tourism Agency – page 32
Old Rectory Hotel, Chris & Sally Entwistle – page 24
Ordnance Survey, map reproduced from Ordnance Survey mapping on behalf of Her Majesty's Stationery Office © Crown Copyright 100000230/2005
P & O Cruises – page 78
Port Aventura – page 113
Premier Holidays Limited – 46
Ramsgate Costumed Walks, Ramsgate Tourist Information Centre – page 35
Ryanair – page 60
Saga – page 80
Salmon Picture Company, Postcard copyright The Salmon Picture Company © – page 3
Sandringham, By Gracious Permission of Her Majesty the Queen – page 30
Sefton Council, www.visitsouthport.com – page 115
Springboard UK – pages 56, 58, 80
Star UK, www.staruk.org.uk – pages 9, 10, 12
Sunday Times © NI Syndication, London, 5 September 2004 – page 99
Tourism South East (Welcome Host) – pages 52–3
Virgin Trains – page 87
VisitBritain – page 27
Waddesdon Manor – page 28
World Tourism Organisation – page 4
World Trade Organisation – page 11
York Hospitality Association – page 65

Photo Acknowledgements

Alamy – pages 14, 30, 38, 101 (top), 102 (top), 105, 117
British Airways – page 2
British Waterways – page 38
Dubailand – page 102 (bottom)
Empics – page 126
Getty/Robert Harding – page 109
Getty News and Sport – pages 78, 101
Milepost 92 $\frac{1}{2}$ – page 76
P&O Stena Line – page 16
The Palm/Nakheel – page 102 (middle)
John Smith – page 105, 108
TUI UK Ltd – page 56

Introduction

Travel and tourism is a very exciting industry. You might be surprised at the range of opportunities for employment within the industry, or for further study if you proceed to the A2 level. As the industry is also growing rapidly, there is likely to be an increase in the employment opportunities open to you.

About the OCR qualification

By studying for this qualification, you will gain an understanding of the skills employers in the travel and tourism industry are looking for, and you will have an opportunity to develop skills in information technology, communication and application of number – as well as working as part of a team and developing your own performance. If you are working towards Key Skills, many of the tasks you undertake will help you develop those skills. The OCR qualification itself may also complement your work for other AS levels, such as Geography, and if you are studying languages you will find that these are very relevant within the travel and tourism industry.

The AS course should help you to:

* develop your interest in travel and tourism, the issues affecting the industry and their potential effects on employment opportunities

* assess the scale and importance of the industry, and of the interrelationships between its components

* appreciate the huge importance of customers to the industry

* develop relevant practical and technical skills

* observe the global and dynamic nature of the industry, how people, environments and issues change, and how the industry responds to these changes

* gain an understanding of the impact of information and communication technology (ICT) on the future development of the industry

* appreciate the significance of the values and attitudes of key stakeholders

* develop your own values and attitudes in relation to travel and tourism issues

* use skills of research, evaluation and problem-solving.

As the course leading to the OCR qualification is vocational, it is very important that you actually have an opportunity to participate in the industry. This may be through a work placement, a part-time job, or by participating in visits to travel and tourism organisations and destinations. At the end of the course the knowledge, understanding and skills you have developed should assist you in gaining employment at operational level in direct contact with customers. You might decide to progress to the Advanced GCE course after successful completion of the AS.

Understanding the marking scheme

You will notice that the assessment evidence grids in the specification for units 2 and 3 have three mark bands for each Assessment Objective. These are all progressive, so to reach the second mark band you need to make sure you have addressed all the points in the first mark band and used the specification to guide you as to the content. Marks are awarded for each Assessment Objective according to your level of performance, then the totals for each Assessment Objective are added together to give a final marks score for that unit. You may achieve quite high marks for one of the objectives, but fewer marks for another, but it is your total marks for the unit that will be used to decide your final grade for the whole qualification.

As an example of this scoring, consider the assessment evidence grid for unit 2, Customer Service.

* If your work for AO1 has explained how the needs of both internal and external customers are met by your chosen organisation, and you have also given a thorough comparison of how

internal and external customer needs are met by that organisation (covering all the types of customers identified in the specification), you might achieve *13 marks* for AO1.

* In AO2, however, your evidence for providing customer service might be weak, showing little understanding of customer service skills and personal presentation, or you might have failed to handle a problem or complaint well. So you could be awarded just *3 marks* for AO2.

* Going on to AO3, you might have undertaken clearly identified research from a number of sources and shown ability to analyse the results of this to explain the effectiveness of the organisation's customer service, so achieving *6 marks* for AO3.

* Then, for AO4, there was some attempt at evaluation showing strengths and weaknesses in the organisation's provision of customer service, but recommendations for improvement were very basic so you might score just *2 marks* for AO4.

Your total marks for this unit would therefore be 13 + 3 + 6 + 2, making 24 out of a possible 50.

About this book

This book has been prepared to help you understand the units of the OCR qualification. There is a chapter for each of the units covered within the qualification, written by senior examiners and moderators who have been involved with the development of the units. Each chapter will give you the relevant knowledge required for that unit, with lots of activities and discussion points to help you develop this understanding and apply it to various situations. There is also guidance given as to what is required for the assessment of the unit.

Each chapter links very closely to the OCR specification. The 'What You Need to Learn' section of the specification is mirrored in the presentation of the units, so it will be easy for you to ensure you have covered all the knowledge elements. It is advisable to work through each

unit thoroughly, rather than 'dropping into' a section – you might not then see the whole picture and your understanding will not be as thorough. To gain higher marks in the assessment (whether it is examination or portfolio) you will need to demonstrate a thorough understanding of that particular unit in the evidence you present to examiners or moderators.

Special features of this book

* **Think it over** is designed to provoke discussion on issues arising as you study.

* **Case studies** will give you an insight into real events and people you may encounter and provide opportunities for discussion in your class groups.

* **Theory into practice** activities are opportunities to work with others and implement the knowledge you will gain as you work through each unit.

* **Assessment guidance** tells you more specifically how you can meet the evidence requirements for the unit.

* **Knowledge check** is there to aid your revision.

* **Resources** are pointers to further information sources and study.

Keep up to date!

At the time of writing this book, all the information was current and relevant. However, travel and tourism is a very dynamic industry and subject to many changes. Hotel groups may be taken over, organisations may change their names or logos, governments may pass new regulations which affect the industry, and so on. It is important that you not only use the information within this book but also keep up to date with developments. You will need to discuss issues with employers in the industry, as well as reading relevant articles in the daily, weekend and trade press to ensure that you are aware of these developments and how they affect the industry as a whole.

Enjoy your studies!

UNIT 1

Introducing travel and tourism

Introduction

This unit sets the scene for your programme of study for the GCE Travel and Tourism qualification. It is an important unit as it lays the foundation for study in many of the other units for the qualification.

This unit will provide an overarching understanding of one of the world's fastest-growing industries. You will investigate the reasons for the rapid growth in the modern travel and tourism industry and understand why it is commonly referred to as 'the world's biggest industry'. You will learn that the UK travel and tourism industry is made up of a wide variety of commercial and non-commercial organisations that interact to supply products and services to tourists. You will develop appreciation of the different values and attitudes of these organisations in travel and tourism. You will learn about the present significance of the industry to the UK economy.

Within this unit you will be able to develop vocational skills related to the travel and tourism industry – in particular, selecting and interpreting appropriate data, problem-solving and understanding and applying industry-related terminology.

How you will be assessed

The unit is assessed by an external examination of two hours' duration. Before the exam you will receive case study materials, which you can use to prepare thoroughly for the test.

What you need to learn

* the nature of travel and tourism
* the scale of the travel and tourism industry
* the development of the modern travel and tourism industry
* the structure of the travel and tourism industry.

The nature of travel and tourism

'Travel and tourism' covers the whole picture of people travelling away from home, whether for business or for leisure, as well as the industry that supports these activities. Right at the beginning you need to understand basic definitions of 'travel' and 'tourism'.

Tourism is defined by the Tourism Society as *'the temporary short-term movement of people to destinations outside the place where they normally live and work, and activities during their stay at these destinations; it includes movement for all purposes, as well as day visits and excursions'*.

Think it over ...

Use as many different sources as possible to find definitions for 'travel' and for 'tourism'. One obvious source is this book, but also use a dictionary and other sources. On the basis of all those definitions, devise *your own* definition of the two terms.

Think it over ...

Discuss these statements, to decide whether they are true or false. Answers are given on page 11.

- The majority of travel and tourism in the world is international.

- The most common method of travel for leisure purposes is by air.

- Tourism is only about leisure holidays.

- Getting a job in the travel and tourism industry means that you will have the chance to see the world.

In 1879, Robert Louis Stevenson wrote in *Travels with a Donkey*: 'For my part, I travel not to go anywhere, but to go. I travel for travel's sake. The great affair is to move.' Some people today still travel for the enjoyment of the travelling, but mostly travel is considered to be how people get to their chosen destination and how they move around the area once they are there.

There are many methods of travelling, including by aircraft, private car, coach, train and boat. We shall be looking at these methods of transportation later in the unit.

Think it over ...

Think about your own experiences:

- Where did you go on holiday last?

- Was it in the UK or abroad?

- How did you travel?

- What type of accommodation did you stay in?

- What did you eat and drink?

- What activities did you do on holiday?

- How was the holiday organised/booked?

Thinking about these things will help you to learn travel and tourism terminology.

You must remember that the travel and tourism industry is dynamic, so you must keep up to date with changes, both locally and nationally. Businesses change hands as well as their names, which can easily lead to confusion. New legislation comes into force that affects the industry, and industry statistics need updating each year. The resources section on page 49 should assist you in understanding the travel and tourism industry at the time of your studies.

Main types of tourism

Tourists can be classified according to where they come from. They can be domestic, inbound or outbound.

Domestic tourism

Domestic tourism involves residents of a country travelling only within their own country. This is generally an easy form of tourism, as there are no language, currency or documentation barriers. Domestic tourism in the United Kingdom was traditionally based at seaside destinations such as Blackpool and Great Yarmouth.

In 2002, expenditure in the United Kingdom on domestic tourism was estimated to be nearly £61 billion. In that year, UK residents took:

* 101.7 million holidays of one night or more, spending £17.4 billion

* 23.3 million overnight business trips, spending £5.6 billion

* 39.6 million overnight trips, spending £3.4 billion.

> **Key term**
>
> Many domestic tourists in the UK now favour the **short break**. This is usually a weekend or mid-week break of three nights or less.

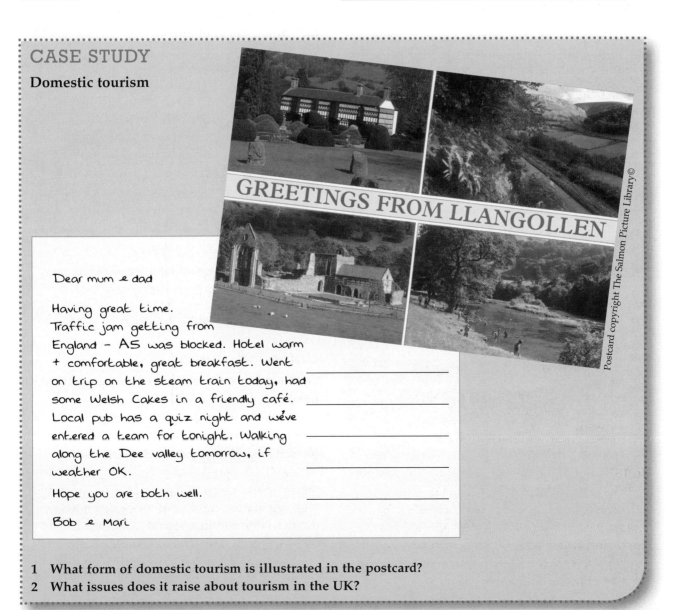

CASE STUDY

Domestic tourism

GREETINGS FROM LLANGOLLEN

Postcard copyright The Salmon Picture Library©

Dear mum & dad

Having great time.
Traffic jam getting from
England – A5 was blocked. Hotel warm
+ comfortable, great breakfast. Went
on trip on the steam train today, had
some Welsh cakes in a friendly café.
Local pub has a quiz night and we've
entered a team for tonight. Walking
along the Dee valley tomorrow, if
weather OK.

Hope you are both well.

Bob & Mari

1 What form of domestic tourism is illustrated in the postcard?
2 What issues does it raise about tourism in the UK?

Inbound tourism

Inbound tourism involves overseas residents visiting the UK. In 2003, the UK ranked sixth in the international tourism earnings league, behind the USA, Spain, France, Italy and Germany.

The 24.7 million overseas visitors who came to the UK in 2003 spent £11.9 billion. Figure 1.1 shows the number of inbound tourists to the UK from various countries, and the amount of money they spent here.

COUNTRY	VISITS (000)	COUNTRY	SPEND (£M)
USA	3 346	USA	2 315
France	3 073	Germany	820
Germany	2 611	France	694
Irish Republic	2 488	Irish Republic	681
Netherlands	1 549	Australia	535

Source: World Tourism Organisation

Figure 1.1 The top five overseas markets for the UK in 2003

Think it over ...

1 Why do you think inbound tourists come to the UK from the USA and the Irish Republic?

2 Do you think the reasons are different for visitors from France, Germany and the Netherlands?

3 Why do you think inbound tourists from Australia make the top five in terms of expenditure?

4 Why should the UK encourage inbound tourism from these countries, especially the USA? (You may wish to work out the average spend per visitor.)

Theory into practice

You are an incoming tour operator serving the needs of the US market. You have been approached by a specialist tour operator, George Busch, of Busch Tours, Fort Lauderdale, Florida. He is interested in bringing groups to your area of the country, and has written to you to ask which local towns may be of interest to the older Florida residents.

Select one town you consider might be suitable. Undertake an evaluation of its attractions, amenities and accessibility for this customer. Write a business letter explaining the attractiveness of the destination, and its suitability for the market.

CASE STUDY

UKinbound

UKinbound (www.ukinbound.co.uk) is the official trade body representing UK inbound tourism. The association represents over 250 major companies and organisations in all areas of travel and tourism. Each month the association produces a Business Barometer which compares visitor numbers and booking forecasts with the previous year. The figures for August 2004 showed a 3.8 per cent increase in *inbound* visitor numbers.

Visit the UKinbound website to get up-to-date figures on inbound visitors.

Outbound tourism

Outbound tourism refers to UK residents taking holidays outside the UK.

Think it over ...

In 1870, the Reverend F. Kilvert wrote in his diary: 'Of all noxious animals, too, the most noxious is a tourist. And of all tourists the most vulgar, ill-bred, offensive and loathsome is the British tourist.'

Discuss whether British tourists are still considered to be badly behaved while on holiday abroad.

Outbound tourism can be classified in the following ways (the terms are explained below):

* inclusive tours or independent tours
* method of transport to leave the UK (air, sea or Channel Tunnel)
* length of holiday – short break of less than four nights or longer holidays
* short haul or long haul
* season of departure – summer or winter.

Key terms

An **inclusive tour** is another name for a package holiday. **Independent tours** are any form of travel that is not part of a package holiday, when travellers put their own itinerary together.
Short-haul destinations are usually in continental Europe, under four hours' flight time away from the UK. **Long-haul destinations** are those beyond Europe, such as Australia, the Far East, the USA and India.

Visits abroad are classified as visits for a period of less than 12 months by people permanently resident in the UK (who may be of foreign nationality).

Since the 1970s the most popular type of holiday abroad has been the inclusive tour by air – the package holiday – lasting more than four nights, taken in the summer to short-haul Mediterranean destinations.

Theory into practice

Carry out a survey in your class and year group.

1 In the last two years, which short-haul destinations have been visited?

2 What destinations were for short breaks? Which were for longer holidays?

3 In the last two years, which long-haul destinations have been visited?

Plot these places on a map. Which are the most popular? Why do you think these were the most popular?

CASE STUDY

Outbound tourism to the USA

A recent study by the US Department of Commerce has shown that shopping is the favourite activity in the USA for travellers from the UK. The research identified two distinct types of shoppers: cultural and leisure.

Cultural shoppers tend to be independent travellers, staying in city centres, who are willing to use public transport, take domestic flights and visit local cultural attractions. Their number one destination is New York City.

Leisure shoppers spend slightly less and favour holidays staying in one place, particularly Orlando. US malls and department stores have always been better value than their UK counterparts – and if the pound is strong in comparison with the dollar, items appear even more of a bargain. Virgin Holidays offers a private fashion show breakfast at Bloomingdale's in New York which gets clients into the store before it opens, gives a preview of the latest season's products, and offers a 10 per cent discount on purchases.

What other packages can be offered to outbound tourists looking for special interest holidays? To get you started, think about winter sports holidays in the Alps.

Main reasons why people travel

From all the many reasons why people travel, we shall be looking at leisure travel, visiting friends and relatives (VFR) and business travel. It is important to observe the differences between these, as the characteristics of each purpose of travel will be different.

Leisure travel

Leisure travel is the most common type and covers holidays, short breaks and day visits to tourist attractions – it therefore includes all 'recreational travel'. Leisure travellers are usually concerned about price. Lower prices will lead to an increase in the number of travellers, and may encourage others to change to destinations they consider are better value for money.

Think it over ...

You have already thought about your recent leisure travel destinations on holidays abroad. Now find out the places in the UK that have been visited on day trips by members of the group. Remember this may include visiting friends and relatives.

Business travel

Business travel includes all travel for business purposes. This may be a meeting, conference, exhibition or trade fair. Business travellers will have little choice in their destination or timing of the trip. Business trips frequently have to be arranged at short notice and are for specific and brief periods. Business travellers will need the convenience of frequent, regular transport, efficient service and good facilities at their destination. Because the company will be paying for all the travel arrangements, rather than the individual, the business traveller will be less concerned about the cost of travelling.

Think it over ...

Discuss in your group the different requirements of business and leisure travellers.

Visiting friends and relatives

Visiting friends and relatives includes such travel as visiting grandparents for a day, or staying with friends for a week. Although people usually stay free of charge when doing this, they do spend money on goods and services in the area they are visiting, such as on food, entertainment and local transport.

Unique characteristics of the travel and tourism industry

The main characteristics of the travel and tourism industry today are varied. It is dominated by small and medium-sized businesses. The industry is dynamic and entrepreneurial in nature. The travel and tourism industry is primarily a 'people business'. This is covered fully in unit 2.

The industry is also characterised by:

* seasonality
* intangibility
* perishability.

Seasonality

Key term

Tourism demand regularly fluctuates over the course of a year. This is known as **seasonality**.

Seasonality is often the result of changes in climate over the year, so a destination that is attractive because of its beaches and hot summers is likely to have a highly seasonal demand. Seasonality also applies to a ski resort that has suitable snow for only part of the year. There are other factors besides climate that influence seasonality, such as the timing of school and work holidays, or regular special events held at a destination.

Seasonality causes major problems for the travel and tourism industry. As it is a service industry the product cannot be stored, so a hotel room that remains unbooked, an empty seat on a flight or an unsold theatre ticket are all lost income to the organisation.

Attempts can be made to reduce the impact of seasonality. One way is to create or move demand to the 'shoulder' or 'trough' months (times of reduced demand), either through reducing prices at these times or by providing all-year facilities. Those who are able to travel at that time of year, such as the retired, may be specifically targeted.

Seasonality also affects travel and tourism organisations over a single week. For example, hotels often experience differences in room bookings at weekends compared with weekdays. This is especially the case when the hotel is filled with business travellers during the week at high rates and achieves a lesser level of room occupancy at the weekend with short-break special offers. Visitor attractions often attract more visitors at weekends than on weekdays.

Look at Figure 1.2, a leaflet advertising Billing Aquadrome.

1 What was the duration of the 2004 season?

2 When is high season and when is low season?

3 At what times of the year are a greater number of bookings expected? How does the leaflet illustrate this?

4 When are cars and motorbikes charged for entry on a daily rate?

5 Why do you think facilities such as Billing Aquadrome operate on a seasonal basis?

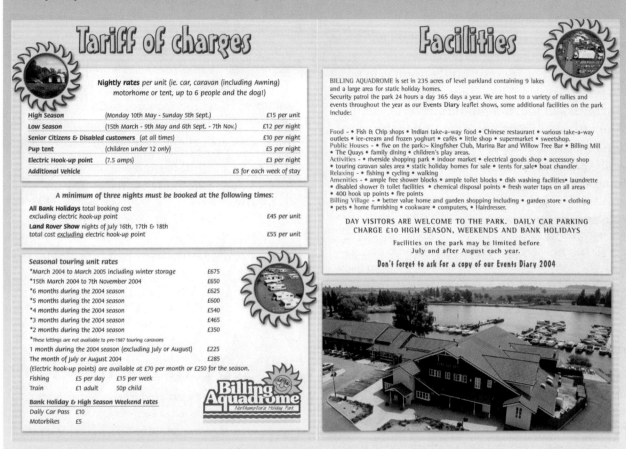

Figure 1.2 Billing Aquadrome: a study of seasonality

Collect a selection of holiday brochures. Look at the pricing panels for the holidays. How does the change in pricing reflect seasonality?

Intangibility

It has often been said that selling holidays is like selling dreams. Travel and tourism is a service rather than a tangible good. 'Tangible' means that you can touch it, but travel and tourism is intangible – you cannot feel a holiday!

This intangibility produces problems for people whose job it is to sell travel and tourism. You cannot, for example, inspect a holiday before you buy it, unlike a car that you can take for a test drive. As a purchaser of a package holiday you can only take on trust what is said or printed about the holiday. This can be a problem as holidays are one of the most expensive purchases made throughout a year. When you buy a package holiday abroad, you are buying more than a simple collection of services, such as an airline seat, hotel room, meals and the opportunity to sit on a sunny beach. You are also buying the temporary use of a different environment, plus the culture and heritage of the region as well as other intangible benefits such as service, atmosphere and hospitality. The planning and anticipation of such a holiday may be as much a part of its enjoyment as the trip itself. Recalling the experience later and looking at photos and videos are a continuation of the experience.

The challenge in travel and tourism is to make the dream equal to the reality. This is difficult as the travel and tourism product tends to vary in standard and quality over time and under different circumstances. A package tour in which you experience bad weather can change an enjoyable experience into a nightmare.

Think it over ...

How has new technology, such as DVDs and the Internet, attempted to overcome the intangibility of travel and tourism? Think about virtual tours and interactive holiday brochures.

Perishability

Perishability is a feature of all travel and tourism products. This means that service products such as tourism, unlike goods, cannot be stored for sale on a future occasion.

For example, a hotel bed or an airline seat unsold, or a conference centre left empty, means lost revenue. This demonstrates the high-risk nature of the travel and tourism industry. Complex pricing and promotion policies need to be devised in an attempt to sell 'off-season' periods.

Weak demand is not the only problem, as travel and tourism is characterised by hotels, airlines, attractions, museums etc., all of which have fixed capacity with a maximum upper level. In peak periods the industry often has difficulty in coping with demand and so charges premium prices or uses queuing as a control mechanism. It is a skill to try to smooth out demand by offering, for example, off-peak prices at theme

parks. Airlines try to sell surplus seats by offering a *standby fare*. This is a discounted rate offered to travellers who are prepared to turn up without booking in advance, in the hope that there will a spare seat.

CASE STUDY

Hotels

Hotels use two statistics to measure their success, and these illustrate perishability. These statistics are (a) the level of occupancy and (b) the average achieved room rate. The latter is the price achieved on rooms sold, and bears little resemblance to the full advertised price or 'rack rate'. Typically most rooms are sold at a discount to rack rate.

1 **Find out rack rates and actual room rates for hotels belonging to chains in your locality.**
2 **At what time of the week are these discounted rates?**
3 **Can you offer an explanation as to why the rooms are reduced at these times?**

The scale of the travel and tourism industry

This part of the unit investigates the scale of the industry at local and national levels. You will be developing skills in order to analyse the most commonly used statistics in travel and tourism.

Consumer spending in the UK on travel and tourism

When you are on holiday or on a day trip you spend money. This may be on food and drink, entrance fees, shopping for souvenirs or fuel to get you there.

The balance of payments

Travel and tourism makes an important contribution to the UK's balance of payments –

that is, the difference between what is imported to the UK and what is exported. It is difficult to assess the true contribution that travel and tourism makes, owing to the intangible nature of the industry, and the fact that people pay for a service rather than a tangible product.

Generally, the money received from visitors to the UK can be considered as an export because it earns foreign currency and brings money into the UK economy. The money spent overseas by outgoing tourists from the UK can be considered as an import because money is taken out of the UK economy. If the value of exports is greater than imports there is a surplus on the balance of payments. If the imports are greater than the exports there is a deficit on the balance of payments.

Currently the amount of tourism export earnings is in deficit – there is more outgoing tourism than incoming tourism. In 2002, there was a record deficit of £15.2 billion, which was £1.2 billion more than in 2001. In 2002, for every £1 spent in the UK by other Europeans, UK residents spent £3 in other parts of Europe. This compares with a £1 to £2 ratio in 1982.

Spending on domestic tourism

Domestic tourists in the UK spend money – not as much per head as overseas visitors, but a substantial amount (see Figure 1.3).

	UK	ENGLAND	SCOTLAND	WALES
1995	20 072	14 630	2 793	1 573
1996	22 041	15 763	3 276	1 781
1997	24 137	17 264	3 724	1 626
1998	22 814	16 383	3 490	1 674
1999	25 635	19 106	3 600	1 723
2000	26 133	19 890	3 699	1 654
2001	26 094	20 278	3 412	1 664
2002	26 699	20 787	3 682	1 543

Source: Star UK

Figure 1.3 All domestic tourism spending (£m), 1995 to 2002

Spending in the UK by overseas residents

In 2002, overseas residents spent £11.7 billion in the UK, nearly four times the amount spent in 1982, but £1.1 billion lower than in 2000. As we have seen, this is important for the UK's overall balance of payments. Incoming visitors to an area help to create or sustain jobs. The government benefits as overseas visitors pay VAT and other taxes on a range of products and services. Overseas visitors are likely to use public transport and so help ensure that routes will continue to run. British theatres and the arts benefit especially – the majority of the audiences of West End shows are incoming tourists.

Employment in the industry

Numbers of people employed in travel and tourism

The travel and tourism industry employs a vast number of people, in a wide range of jobs. Employment in the industry in the UK is, in government figures, measured at 2.1 million, which is some 7.4 per cent of all people in employment. Approximately 163 000 of these jobs are in self-employment.

Around 50 000 new jobs are created in travel and tourism each year. There are employment opportunities in travel agencies, tour operators, hospitality providers, airlines, coach companies and tourist attractions.

The dynamic nature of the industry means that permanent, full-time positions are not the norm in travel and tourism employment. Much employment is part-time or short-term contractual, and many jobs operate during unsociable hours (evenings and night-shifts or weekends). The seasonality of the industry means that there are peak times when more people will be employed.

The ability of the travel and tourism industry to create jobs is one of its main economic benefits and is often the main reason why public sector bodies invest in UK tourism. It is estimated that for every one direct job created in travel and tourism, one-half of an indirect job is created elsewhere in the economy.

Employment by category of tourism-related industries

The following Standard Industrial Classification (SIC) codes are used when measuring employment in tourism-related industries:

✳ 551/552 – hotels and other tourist accommodation

✳ 553 – restaurants, cafés etc.

✳ 554 – bars, public houses and nightclubs

✳ 633 – travel agencies and tour operators

✳ 925 – libraries/museums and other cultural activities

✳ 926/927 – sport and other recreation.

Think it over …

Look at Figure 1.4 relating to employment in travel and tourism in the UK in 2001. Why do you think this might not be a full and accurate picture of employment in travel and tourism in the whole of the UK?

	551/552	553	554	633	925	926/927	Total
ENGLAND	269 617	455 810	464 309	113 189	64 490	229 148	1 696 563
Cumbria	6 843	4 409	4 192	549	720	3 013	19 726
Northumbria	9 387	16 618	24 278	3 016	2 637	15 097	71 033
North West	27 858	51 491	64 376	15 814	6 957	38 540	205 036
Yorkshire	23 217	38 094	48 403	6 223	8 373	33 492	157 802
Heart of England	44 272	72 079	102 993	13 532	10 692	61 217	304 785
East of England	25 566	45 383	45 492	12 359	5 172	36 541	170 513
London	48 050	121 630	58 364	34 156	14 689	54 108	330 997
South East	19 538	37 134	36 063	14 454	4 847	27 727	139 764
Southern	26 555	36 650	39 527	7 308	5 119	38 107	153 266
South West	38 330	32 322	40 620	5 778	5 285	21 304	143 639
SCOTLAND	51 330	49 824	40 755	8 855	8 350	38 284	197 398
WALES	17 837	20 730	27 244	3 146	3 908	16 597	89 461
GB	338 783	526 364	532 307	125 190	76 748	384 029	1 983 421

Figures exclude Northern Ireland, and self-employment jobs are excluded.

Source: Star UK

Figure 1.4 Employment in tourism-related industries in 2001

Tourists coming into the UK

The number of visits by overseas residents to the UK more than doubled from 11.6 million visits in 1982 to a peak of 25.7 million in 1998, before falling each year to 22.8 million in 2001. The largest fall of 9.4 per cent occurred in 2001 when there was foot and mouth disease between February and September, and the terrorist attacks in the USA on 11 September.

Think it over ...

The UK is ranked sixth in the world in terms of the number of inbound tourists (see Figure 1.5).

1 Discuss why you think France is the number one destination in the world.

2 Why do you think there was a 6.7 per cent reduction in international visitors to the USA?

3 Which country has the greatest growth in international visitors? Think of reasons why.

RANK		2002	CHANGE 2002/2001	SHARE
1	France	77.0	2.4%	11.0%
2	Spain	51.7	3.3%	7.4%
3	USA	41.9	−6.7%	6.0%
4	Italy	39.8	0.6%	5.7%
5	China	36.8	11.0%	5.2%
6	UK	24.2	5.9%	3.4%
7	Canada	20.1	1.9%	2.9%
8	Mexico	19.7	−0.7%	2.8%
9	Austria	18.6	2.4%	2.6%
10	Germany	18.0	0.6%	2.6%
	World	703	2.7%	100%

Figure 1.5 International tourist arrivals (millions)

Source: World Trade Organisation

Think it over ...

These are suggested answers to the questions asked in the second 'Think it over' box on page 2:
(1) Tourism in the world is mainly domestic travel, accounting for about 80 per cent of tourism trips.
(2) The majority of transport is by surface methods, mainly by car. (3) Tourism includes all types of purposes for a visit, including business and visiting family and friends. (4) Most employment in tourism is in the hospitality sector and involves little travel.

Domestic tourism

Figure 1.6 shows the number of UK residents taking holidays within the UK in 1996 and 2002, and their spending.

TOURIST BOARD REGIONS	1996		2002	
	Number of trips (millions)	Expenditure (£m)	Number of trips (millions)	Expenditure (£m)
United Kingdom	154.2	22 041	167.3	26 699
Northumbria	3.7	402	4.8	868
Cumbria	3.7	503	4.3	728
North West	11.9	1 632	14.5	2 316
Yorkshire	11.9	1 713	12.2	1 595
East of England	15.8	1 860	14.5	1 704
Heart of England	18.9	2 164	24.6	3 166
London	12.9	1 633	16.1	2 818
Southern	11.5	1 586	14.6	2 065
South East England	11.9	1 240	10.9	1 355
South West	17.5	3 029	21.0	3 901
England	117.3	15 763	134.9	20 787
Wales	13.6	1 781	11.9	1 543
Scotland	19.6	3 276	18.5	3 683
Northern Ireland	3.8	698	2.8	525

Source: Star UK

Figure 1.6 UK residents taking holidays in the UK in 1996 and 2002

Theory into practice

1 Locate each of the regional tourist boards represented in Figure 1.6 on a map of the United Kingdom.

2 Which regional tourist board area had the greatest number of domestic trips to it in 1996 and 2002? Research this tourist board area to find out the attractions visitors would want to see.

3 Which regional tourist board area had the greatest domestic spending in 1996 and 2002? Research this tourist board region to find out what domestic visitors might be spending their money on.

4 Why do you think the regional tourist board with the most trips is different from that with the most spending?

Domestic tourism trends

The travel and tourism market has been unstable in recent years with a number of unforeseen events having an impact on the domestic market. These include:

* fuel blockades at UK petrol stations
* the restrictions imposed on the rail network after the Hatfield disaster
* the events of 11 September 2001
* the foot-and-mouth outbreak.

Despite the instability caused by these events, the underlying trend in the demand for domestic tourism continues to grow. The increasing interest in travel as a leisure activity, the fall in the real cost of travelling, and the change in modern lifestyles are all factors that are driving demand for holidays. The growth in multi-holidaymaking has stimulated the market for short holidays in the UK, while long holidays in the UK have remained more or less constant.

Theory into practice

1 Visit www.staruk.org.uk and locate the section on domestic tourism trends.

2 Analyse these statistics. Look specifically at the different trends in holiday tourism, business tourism and VFR.

3 Try to explain the patterns in the trends.

Outbound tourists

UK residents taking holidays outside the UK

A record 59.4 million visits were made abroad in 2002, nearly three times the number in 1982. The amount of spending was also a record in 2002, at £27.0 billion.

Of all the visits in 2002, 39.9 million were holiday visits (that is, two-thirds of the total). Over half of these were package holidays.

Continental Europe was the most popular region for UK residents to visit, accounting for 74 per cent of all visits but only 57 per cent of total spending. For the first time, Spain became the most popular country visited with 12.5 million trips – beating France as a destination by just 0.4 million visits.

Why the big increase in outbound tourism?

The growth in the value of sterling compared with other currencies has had a positive effect on outbound holidays, which are growing at a faster rate than domestic holidays.

UK consumers expect more choice, variety and individuality than ever before. Although mass-market sun and sea holidays are still the majority of the outbound holiday market, it is specialist holidays targeted at particular market segments that are the key to profitability. Many of the major outbound tour operators offer a range of different product brands targeted at different markets.

The main reason for the underlying growth in the UK holiday market is the increasing level of repeat purchases or multi-holidaymaking in any year. However, since 1999, the percentage of UK adults taking an annual holiday has not changed significantly.

Outbound holiday growth has been much more dynamic than domestic holiday growth, with long and short holidays each showing increases. Much of the growth in short holidays abroad has been stimulated by the establishment and expansion of low-cost airline services. These services are characterised by direct independent booking facilities via the Internet. Their operation has encouraged a growth in the use of the Internet for seeking information on travel and for booking transport and accommodation.

Travel arrangements of outbound tourists

Travelling by air was the most popular mode of transport and accounted for 74 per cent of all visits. Travelling by sea was the next most popular mode, accounting for 17 per cent of visits. The Channel Tunnel was used for the remaining visits (9 per cent).

Spending of outbound tourists

On average, air travellers spent the most money per visit (£519), while those travelling by sea or the Channel Tunnel spent far lower amounts (£339 and £277 respectively). These differences were due to a number of factors, including variations in the reason for the visit, the length of stay and the region of the world visited.

The average spending per visit ranged from £348 for VFR, to £528 for business trips. The average spending on holidays was £465.

Why do UK residents travel abroad?

As you have already read, two-thirds of visits made by UK residents were to go on holiday, making this the most popular reason for travelling abroad. More than half (52 per cent) of these holidays were taken as an inclusive tour. Business trips and VFR were the next most popular reasons for travelling abroad.

Think it over …

What are the implications for the UK economy of the continued increase in outbound tourism? Think about the balance of payments.

The development of the modern travel and tourism industry

The growth in international and domestic travel and tourism has been dramatic. Figures from the World Tourism Organisation (WTO – www.world-tourism.org) stated there were 703 million international tourist arrivals in 2002, climbing from 25 million in 1950 and 592 million in 1996. To understand today's travel and tourism industry, you need to know about the major developments in recent times. You have to show you understand the dynamic nature of travel and tourism. This section is about the key factors that have contributed to the dramatic growth in the travel and tourism industry.

Changing socio-economic factors

These factors include:

* changes in car ownership
* increasing leisure time
* an increase in disposable income
* the impact of the national economy.

Car ownership

Car ownership has increased dramatically in the last 50 years. This is because the income of people has risen and cars are more affordable to buy and run. In 1970 there were approximately 11 million cars on UK roads, compared with 2.3 million in 1950. Figures from the Department for Transport (www.dft.gov.uk) show that in 2002 there were over 25.5 million private cars in the UK.

This means that car owners have an additional travel option, and can reach destinations that are inaccessible or difficult to reach by public transport. Car owners can also choose *when* to travel without timetable restrictions and the speed of travel – car ownership offers flexibility of travel.

The rise in car ownership has led to a drop in demand for traditional types of public transport, such as trains and coaches for holiday travel. This leads to cuts in services. Another effect of the increase in car ownership in the UK has been the rise in associated environmental problems, such as pollution, congestion and the loss of land to road building programmes.

Think it over …

How many cars are owned by people in your household? What are the cars mainly used for? Try to find out the answers to these questions also for your parents' and grandparents' generations when they were your age. What do these differences show you about increases in car ownership?

Increasing leisure time

The increase in leisure time has come about primarily due to paid holiday entitlement. In the UK we have a number of one-day Bank Holidays

as well as annual leave. Holiday entitlement is partly responsible for the seasonality of travel and tourism, as parents take holidays in the summer to coincide with school holidays.

The 'working week' has also been made shorter, to an average of 37 hours. This has to be compared with the 1950s when a 50-hour working week was normal, including at least half a day on Saturday. Many employers now operate flexitime (flexible working hours), which is of great benefit to the travel and tourism industry, allowing employees to have long weekends and hence take short breaks.

Labour-saving household equipment, such as dishwashers, washing machines and microwaves, mean that household chores can be carried out more quickly, so leading to greater leisure time.

People are on average also living longer and retiring earlier. This so-called 'grey' market is important in travel and tourism, as retired people frequently have the time and money to spend on holidays and other activities.

CASE STUDY

Saga

The Saga group (www.saga.co.uk) has its origins in the 1950s, when the founder of the company, Sidney De Haan, bought his first seaside hotel in Folkestone, Kent. In 1951 he organised a package holiday exclusively for retired people, realising that many would appreciate a quieter off-season break by the sea.

The Saga organisation now aims to serve the 50+ market. It aims to offer excellent value for money and direct booking, fully focusing on and responding to the changing demands of the older target market, which is the fastest growing demographic group in the UK. The product range of Saga covers virtually every holiday type, including those with an historic and/or cultural dimension in the UK and beyond, city breaks, as well as exotic long–haul destinations, adventure holidays and cruises.

Discuss the differences in requirements of the 50+ age group compared with other age groups of holidaymakers.

Disposable income

> **Key term**
>
> **Disposable income** is the household income that is left over when tax, housing and the basics of life have been paid out.

There has been a general trend for UK disposable income to rise, so leading to increased expenditure on leisure activities, including travel and tourism.

The impact of the national economy

The national economic situation affects the travel and tourism industry significantly. When there is enough disposable income in the economy due to high levels of employment, people have on average more money to spend on travel and tourism products and services. This can be measured by the gross national product.

> **Key term**
>
> The **gross national product** (GNP) is the measure of a country's total economic production, calculated by adding the value of all goods and services produced to the net revenue from abroad.

The reverse is also true. When there are high levels of unemployment and little growth, people have on average less disposable income to spend money on travel and tourism.

Technological developments

The travel and tourism industry has developed as a direct result of technological developments. These developments have been in transport technology, such as jet aircraft, improved trains and luxury coaches. There have also been developments in information and communications technology such as the Internet, computer reservation systems (CRS) and global distribution systems (GDS), as well as credit and debit cards which allow customers to pay in more convenient ways.

Developments in transport technology

The most significant development for air travel was the introduction of jet aircraft in the 1950s, particularly the Boeing 707 in 1958. Air travel became fast, safe, comfortable and – relative to previous decades – cheap. The 'jumbo jet' (Boeing 747) introduced in 1969 had several impacts on the travel and tourism industry. It was possible to fly further in less time, so making long-haul destinations more accessible, and the price of air travel was reduced due to the increased capacity of the jumbo jet (400 seats).

It is not just air transport that has been revolutionised by new technology. The Channel Tunnel was opened to passengers in 1995 and led to competition for cross-channel ferry services.

Theory into practice

Using brochures or the Internet, complete the table below to compare the range of methods of travelling across the English Channel. Try to include at least *two* operators for each method.

Method of travel	Operator	Departure point	Arrival point	Journey time	Return fare
Rail					
Sea with own car					
Sea as foot passenger					
Air					

Technological developments in booking systems

Ten years ago travel agents had almost complete control of travel bookings. Customers liked the convenience of a package holiday, and bargain priced beach breaks could often be found displayed in the travel agency window. Using viewdata systems, travel agencies could make direct bookings with tour operators.

Key term

Viewdata consisted of a screen that displayed information transmitted by phone lines. By 1987, 85 per cent of all package holidays were booked through this system.

Then there was the development of CRS technology. Using their computers, travel agents could find out information on destinations that would take you, the customer, dozens of phone calls to uncover. The market leader in the UK for computer reservation systems is Galileo. Other systems are Sabre, Worldspan and Amadeus. Global distribution systems now link up several CRS and present information to the user.

Teletext turned the TV in your sitting room into a shop window, offering late deals at the touch of a remote control and one phone call. The tour operators set up call centres and encouraged you to ring them directly, often at times when high street travel agencies were closed. The explosion of the Internet and of no-frills airlines selling direct to the public meant that travel agents and tour operators no longer had the monopoly on holiday bookings, and everyone thought that they could save time and money by cutting out the travel agent.

The Big Four tour operators (TUI, Thomas Cook, First Choice and MyTravel) bought up dozens of smaller operators and built up huge chains of high street travel agencies, all with the intention of selling as many of their own-brand holidays as possible. The media started forecasting the demise of travel agents, so travel agencies had to *add value* to their sales – either by offering bargains not available elsewhere or by finding ways to provide a superior service.

Changing consumer needs and expectations

Alongside the huge growth in travel and tourism, as outlined in an earlier section, there have been significant changes due to a variety of cultural and social factors. We also now demand higher standards of quality and customer service, a subject covered in detail in unit 2.

The simple sun-and-sea holidays of the 1960s seem to appeal to fewer people today, and more flexibility is demanded. Customers today prefer to choose the type of accommodation, the board basis, the type of transport and the length of the holiday. Package holidays now need to offer this choice.

Special-interest holidays in particular have been developed to cater for a range of interests. Activity and adventure holidays have become increasingly important, especially those that include activities such as white-water rafting or scuba diving.

As leisure time increases and disposable incomes rise, the 'second holiday' has developed. Skiing became popular as a second (winter) holiday from the 1970s, and in the 1980s the short-break market developed. This has benefited the domestic travel and tourism industry. Also, due to low-price air fares and other quick transport methods, the overseas city break is now very popular.

Protecting the environment

The travelling public is becoming more environmentally aware, as we see the damage that can be done to popular holiday destinations. Tour operators have responded to this and many brochures will make a statement about what they are doing to support local communities.

The Travel Foundation (www.thetravelfoundation.org.uk) is a charity that develops practical solutions to help protect and improve holiday destinations. It works in partnership with the UK tourism industry to encourage action to spread the *benefits* of tourism to local communities. First Choice is among the travel companies that asks in its brochure for every customer to make a small voluntary contribution of 10p per adult and 5p per child to the charity when booking a holiday.

Product development and innovation

Package holidays

The origin of the package holiday is credited to a man called Thomas Cook, who took his passengers by train from Loughborough to Leicester in 1841. The modern package, or inclusive tour, was created by Vladimir Raitz, who in 1950 carried a party of thirty-two holidaymakers to Corsica. That package included return flights, transfers, tented accommodation and full board. By chartering a flight and filling every seat he managed to keep the price low. He then established Horizon Holidays and chartered planes to Palma, Malaga and other Mediterranean resorts, carrying 300 passengers in the first year of operation.

Package holidays have since grown with Thomson, Airtours and First Choice being the biggest outgoing tour operators in terms of the number of package holidays sold. Mediterranean destinations are still the most popular with the British, but long-haul destinations including the Caribbean, the USA, the Far East and Australia are becoming increasingly important package holiday destinations as travel costs fall. More information on package holidays can be found later in this chapter.

All-inclusive holidays

'All-inclusives' were introduced by Club Med in the 1950s. All-inclusives can now include all meals, drinks, sports and entertainment, for example, but what is covered in the package does vary between operators. As an example, an all-inclusive package with First Choice at the Occidental Grand Fuerteventura four-star hotel in Jandia included the following:

* Food – buffets for breakfast, lunch and dinner; unlimited snacks 10 a.m. to midnight; afternoon tea and cakes; picnics available on request; unlimited ice cream between 3 p.m. and 6 p.m.

* Drink – unlimited locally produced alcoholic drinks between 10.30 a.m. and midnight for adults; unlimited soft drinks, tea, coffee and mineral water between 10 a.m. and midnight.

Theory into practice

Collect a number of brochures, or use the Internet, to find five all-inclusive packages. Compare the packages to find out exactly what is on offer as part of the deal. Which package do you think offers the best deal?

Holiday camps

Holiday camps are purpose-built complexes providing family accommodation and a range of entertainment facilities on site for a relatively low, all-inclusive price. They were pioneered by Billy Butlin in the 1930s, who opened his first camp at Skegness on the Lincolnshire coast in 1936. Holiday camps worked on the principle that if children were happy on holiday, then the parents would be too. Butlin's, Pontin's and Warner's became market leaders in this type of holiday.

In recent years they have modified these camps to meet changing consumer needs and expectations. New types of holiday centre, such as Center Parcs, have evolved.

Theory into practice

Research changes that have occurred in the holiday camp and holiday centre sector of the industry in the past 50 years. Why did these changes happen? Do you foresee further changes in the next few years?

External factors

Legislation

Key term

Legislation consists principally of Acts of Parliament passed by central government. Local authorities can introduce by-laws that apply only locally.

The Holidays with Pay Act 1938

This encouraged voluntary agreements by employers on paid holidays and generated the idea of a two-week paid holiday for all workers. Although this ambition was not fulfilled until several years after the end of the Second World War, by 1939 some 11 million of the UK's 19 million workforce were entitled to paid holidays, a key factor in generating mass travel and tourism.

Countryside and Rights of Way Act 2000

This Act (referred to as 'CROW') made it lawful for the public to enter areas that were previously restricted to the landowners. In England, the public will have 'open access' to around one million hectares (4000 square miles, 8 per cent of the country). The right does not include cycling, horse riding, driving a vehicle or camping, and there are various other rules to protect the land and the interests of the landowners, such as farmers.

Theory into practice

The Countryside Agency provides details of the new legislation on its website (www.countryside.gov.uk). Use the website to attempt to answer the following questions.

1 When was the major new right of access introduced?

2 What activities are people permitted, and not permitted, to do on all land?

3 What type of land is being opened up due to CROW?

4 What discretion do landowners have?

5 What are the main points of the Countryside Code?

Development of Tourism Act 1968

This established the British Tourist Authority (BTA), which was set up to encourage incoming tourism from overseas visitors, as well as the four national tourist boards (NTB) of England, Scotland, Wales and Northern Ireland which oversee tourism in their own areas. The BTA and the NTBs were given the power and authority to act in the name of the government and to promote British tourism. Since 2004 the BTA and the English Tourism Council have been merged into VisitBritain.

Each NTB works within its own country to encourage and improve amenities for travel and tourism. They offer information services, undertake research and provide grants for tourism-related projects. In order to extend their influence within their countries, each NTB sets up Regional Tourist Boards. You can find more information on NTBs and regional tourist boards later in this chapter (see page 35).

EU Directive on Package Travel 1995

This ensures that customers of package holiday providers have financial protection. If a company fails, customers who have not yet travelled can get their money back. Those on holiday at the time do not have to pay additional costs.

The Directive places a number of duties on the organisers of package holidays, including providing clear contract terms, giving emergency telephone numbers, providing a variety of compensation options if the agreed services are not supplied, producing accurate promotional materials including brochures, as well as providing proof that the organiser has security against insolvency.

Disability Discrimination Act 1995

This came about through public pressure to persuade people and businesses to remove the barriers facing people with disabilities.

Key term

In terms of this Act, **disability** means a physical or mental impairment that has a substantial and long-term adverse effect on a person's ability to carry out normal day-to-day activities.

Travel and tourism organisations such as visitor attractions have to be accessible to those with restricted mobility or in wheelchairs. Public transport providers have been encouraged to adapt their vehicles with facilities to make it easier for people with disabilities to use their service, for example by fitting low steps on to buses. Commercially, all adaptations can be seen as a positive move, as there are 10 million disabled people in the UK with a spending power of £48 million.

The Act came fully into force in October 2004. It requires travel agents to make 'reasonable' adjustments to their shops to ensure that disabled people can have access to their facilities and services. If adjustments to the premises are not made, the travel agency can be sued and required to pay compensation.

Health and Safety at Work Act 1974

This applies to workers in all areas of travel and tourism. It can be summarised as follows.

* Employers have a general duty to provide for the health, safety and welfare of those they employ. Employers are also required to consult employees about health and safety arrangements and prepare a written health and safety policy statement.

* Employers need to ensure that their operations do not put non-employees (such as customers) at risk.

* Adequate information about any work-related hazards and the precautions needed to contain them must be made available.

* All employees have to take reasonable care to ensure their own health and safety at work and that of other people who might be affected by their actions.

Other relevant legislation

Other legislation that applies to travel and tourism includes:

* Control of Substances Hazardous to Health Regulations 1999 (COSHH)

* Health and Safety (First Aid) Regulations 1981

* Data Protection Act 1998

* Food Safety Act 1990
* Adventure Activities Licensing Regulations 1996
* Trade Description Act 1968
* Consumer Protection Act 1987
* Sale of Goods Act 1979 and the Sale and Supply of Goods Act 1994.

This is not a complete list. Much of this legislation specifically applies to the travel and tourism industry, and you will be studying many of these in other areas of your course.

CASE STUDY

Lost bags

From September 2004, travellers are entitled to far higher levels of compensation if an airline loses, delays or damages their luggage. The UK is now bound by the terms of the 1999 Montreal Convention, which bases claims on the value of a bag's contents. Previously passengers relied on the Warsaw Convention, which based claims on luggage weight, regardless of contents. Now, if a 20kg bag is lost on a flight to New York, the maximum compensation travellers are entitled to is £807, compared with £276 beforehand.

1 **Collect newspaper articles on legislation relating to travel and tourism.**
2 **For each one, summarise how it benefits travellers.**

The role of local authorities and government

Local government has a part to play in providing tourism facilities for both local people and visitors to the area.

Local councils are also responsible for providing services such as litter bins, toilets, car and coach parking. Primarily these services are provided for local people who have elected the council but, particularly in tourist centres and seaside resorts, the council will take into account the needs of visitors. Local government also works in collaboration with the private sector, as planning permission will need to be sought for any building or development in the area.

Fluctuations in currency

Exchange rates have always been an important factor in the rise, or fall, of the travel and tourism industry. If there is a rise in the value of sterling compared with other currencies, outbound tourism tends to increase as travellers know they will receive more for their money abroad. Exchange rates obviously depend on the strength or weakness of sterling, but they are also affected by the internal strengths of currencies in the main destination countries.

Theory into practice

You can find up-to-date exchange rates from many sources – TV text, the Internet, foreign exchange bureaux and newspapers. Keep a record of the sterling exchange rates for the euro, the US dollar and the Australian dollar over a period of a few weeks. What changes have happened in the exchange rates over the period? What does this mean for outbound UK travellers?

Climatic change

Climate plays a crucial role in how people use their leisure time. In the UK there are marked differences in climate, with the west and south generally experiencing warmer summers and less severe winters than the north. You will probably be aware of the debate over global warming and climate change.

Natural disasters

In 2004, three major hurricanes affected the Caribbean and Florida, Japan was lashed by typhoons, and China coped with mud slides and floods. There was an ice storm in Sydney and enough torrential rain in New York to disrupt the US Open Tennis. The summer in the UK was the wettest since 1912, with some rivers bursting their banks. There was severe flooding in the Cornish village of Boscastle, leading to considerable damage to property, and the midlands, northern and eastern England suffered twice their average August rainfall. These are the types of natural disaster that can disrupt the travel and tourism industry.

CASE STUDY

Ivan the Terrible

In early September 2004, the third hurricane in a month affected the Caribbean and Florida in the USA. Hurricanes Charley and Frances had already rampaged through Florida, killing 50 people and creating £5 billion of storm damage. Theme parks were shut and coastal areas evacuated.

Ivan was a category 5 hurricane (the top of the scale). It generated 156mph winds. It devastated 90 per cent of buildings on its rampage across Grenada, an island supposedly outside the hurricane belt.

Jamaica's southern shore was affected by waves as high as houses, howling winds and horizontal rain. Power lines were torn down, large trees crashed to the ground and rivers running through the capital city, Kingston, overflowed and flooded the streets. Looters went on the prowl. About 2500 British holidaymakers were airlifted from Jamaica to hotels in the Dominican Republic.

The hurricane also left a path of destruction affecting resorts in Cuba, the Cayman Islands, Mexico and Florida. The Federation of Tour Operators estimated that around 10 000 UK holidaymakers in total were caught up in the hurricane.

Additionally, thousands of UK travellers faced disruption or the cancellation of their holidays to the Caribbean and Florida. The Association of British Travel Agents (ABTA) advised anyone travelling to the region to contact their tour operator and airline before leaving for the airport. People whose holiday plans are disrupted have three options: defer their trip; change to an alternative destination; or take a refund. It was the tour operators that covered the substantial cost of repatriating passengers.

Sandals, which has 14 resort hotels in Jamaica, estimated that Hurricane Ivan cost it £3 million in replacement holidays. Its Blue Chip Guarantee means that if a customer's holiday is hit at any time by a hurricane – even on the last day – the operator will provide another completely free of charge.

A technological advancement that was used during the hurricane was text messages on mobile phones. The charter airline Britannia and First Choice Airways kept duty managers informed of hurricane conditions by text messages. Staff on the ground in Florida and the Caribbean received regular updates about the path of the hurricane, plus news of flight cancellations, aircraft swaps and airport closures which they could then pass on to reps and customers. This innovative system replaced pagers, and allowed staff in the UK to send text messages from a computer to numerous phones at once at low cost.

1 **Imagine you are on holiday when a natural disaster affects the area. What would be your main concerns?**
2 **What information would you expect to receive from the organiser of your holiday?**
3 **What information would you expect to receive from the authorities in the area affected?**
4 **How does the case study demonstrate the impact of technological developments in travel and tourism?**

War, civil unrest, terrorism and crime

The travel and tourism industry is vulnerable to war, civil unrest, terrorism and crime. Examples are the war in Iraq, terrorism attacks such as on 11 September 2001, and the nightclub bombs in Bali. Most of these have only a short-term effect on the numbers who travel, but that effect can still result in a huge amount of business lost, and some companies failing.

The Foreign and Commonwealth Office (www.fco.gov.uk) has a section on its website that informs visitors of potential danger areas around the world.

Besides the immediate effects of terrorist attacks on an area, what other effects may these have in the short and long term? Think about this from the point of view of (a) a leisure traveller, (b) a business traveller, (c) a tour operator, (d) an airline, (e) the government of the nation that suffered the attack, and (f) the UK government.

The future

The World Tourism Organisation (WTO) (www.world-tourism.org) produces a report each year on the long-term prospects for tourism. The WTO forecasts that worldwide international arrivals are expected to reach over 1.56 billion by the year 2020. Of these, 1.18 billion will be between regions and 377 million will be long-haul travel. It is predicted that by 2020 the top three tourist receiving regions will be Europe (717 million tourists), East Asia and the Pacific (379 million) and the Americas (282 million), followed by Africa, the Middle East and South Asia.

It is impossible to make precise predictions of the future developments in travel and tourism. The following examples may or may not happen.

Space tourism is a development that is likely to take place over the next few years. The world's first privately financed spacecraft was launched in 2004, and in future space tourists will have the opportunity to travel 62 miles above the earth and stay in a hotel while they are up there. The price charged for such flights is likely to be considerable.

Other developments in transport technology include Airbus's A380 'superjumbo', with 555 seats compared with the 'regular' Boeing 747 jumbo's 415 seats. The first commercial flight, with Singapore Airlines, is scheduled for 2006. Inside the airplane could be fountains, cocktail bars, showers and beds. It will have extra fuel capacity so it has a longer range, making it possible for the first time for a full plane to fly for 14 hours, for example from Melbourne to Los Angeles. Air travel is growing at a rate of 5 per cent each year, so it is likely to double in 15 years and treble in 23 years. The superjumbo will be quieter than the Boeing 747, carry 35 per cent more passengers and burn 12 per cent less fuel per seat.

The Chinese and Russian markets, with a population of 1.3 billion, are likely to produce many new tourists. VisitBritain is expecting the number of visitors from China to the UK to double in the next five years to 130 000, and the number of visitors from Russia to increase by 50 per cent in the same period to more than 200 000. Travel companies are targeting these upcoming markets. The UK is seen as a desirable destination by Russians. Chinese consumers are cost and quality conscious and are less likely to buy on-line as they do not have credit cards.

According to the WTO, China itself is expected to become the world's leading tourism destination by 2020, with some 100 million outbound tourists and 130 million international arrivals each year.

You are an assistant in the Marketing Department of SunScape Tours, a medium-sized tour operator. You have been asked to give the Marketing Manager your views on the growth destinations for the next few years. Your company has largely dealt with the traditional sun, sea and sand tours to the Mediterranean, but is planning to enter the long-haul market. Prepare a report that suggests and justifies the new markets the company should enter.

The structure of the travel and tourism industry

The structure of the travel and tourism industry is complex because it is made up of a wide variety of interrelated commercial and non-commercial organisations. The travel and tourism industry is predominantly led by the private sector, with the majority of enterprises being small and medium-sized. You need to know how these organisations work together and interact to provide the tourist 'experience', and you need to show appreciation of the different values and attitudes of these organisations. The structure of the industry includes:

* commercial organisations
* non-commercial organisations (including public and voluntary sectors)
* agencies delivering travel and tourism products and services.

Figure 1.7 shows that the needs of the visitor are met by a variety of components at a destination. Attractions are often the stimulus for a visit. Transportation both to and from the destination and whilst there ensures accessibility. Accommodation and catering provides places to stay and receive hospitality whilst at the destination. Tourism development and promotion will provide the visitor with information about the destination and activities such as guided tours.

Figure 1.7 Components of a destination area

Theory into practice

1 Select a UK tourist destination you are interested in. It may be a city, seaside resort, countryside area or major attraction. Collect information on the destination, such as promotional leaflets and brochures.

2 Produce a display that illustrates the components that make up the destination.

Commercial organisations

This section looks at the range of *private sector organisations* that make up the travel and tourism industry.

The commercial or private sector of the travel and tourism industry involves business organisations owned by individuals or groups of people. Business organisations in this sector tend to operate for profit. This means that the money the businesses receive from trading (i.e. from selling their goods or services to customers or clients) must be more than is spent on buying stock or providing services.

Profit maximisation may be an overriding priority for some organisations. Survival may also be a distinct aim – for example to survive a downturn in trade in the hope of a better future in the next few years.

More aggressive private sector organisations may aim to increase their market share in direct competition with similar business organisations offering products or services. For example, a travel agency may aim to progress from being a local organisation based in one town to a regional or national company with many branches, by competing with, taking over or merging with other travel agencies.

Another aim might be to maintain a constant cash flow, to keep money flowing into and out of the organisation, and not allowing debts to pile up.

There are five different legal forms of business operating in the private sector in the travel and tourism industry. These are now looked at in greater depth.

Sole trader

This business is owned and controlled by one person. This person takes the risks, provides the capital (perhaps from savings or a loan), keeps the profits or bears the losses. This is known as 'unlimited liability'.

The sole trader is able to employ additional workers if necessary, but is restricted as the business is usually small and cash flow needs to be controlled carefully. Examples of sole trader enterprises in travel and tourism are independent travel agents and owner proprietors of hospitality businesses (e.g. bed and breakfast establishments or fish and chip shops).

Figure 1.8 The Old Rectory

Public limited companies

Public limited companies operate within the UK only, or in several countries as *multinationals*. Examples of public limited companies involved in the travel and tourism industry and listed on the Stock Exchange include Hilton Group, Whitbread, Carnival, Stagecoach, British Airways, Avis Europe, MyTravel, First Choice and Euro Disney. All of these companies are public limited companies and must include 'plc' as part of their name.

Because the share prices of these companies are 'quoted' and the shares are sold openly on the Stock Exchange, you or any member of the public can invest in them.

Ownership control is divided between the shareholders who technically own the company (because they have invested the capital) and the controllers who are the board of directors.

Co-operatives

A co-operative is based on shareholders who own the company. However, the principles involved are more democratic – in a co-operative there is only one vote per shareholder, rather than one vote per share owned.

Partnerships

A partnership means that the ownership of the business is undertaken by several individuals – between two and twenty people.

Since a partnership involves more than one person, there is usually more capital available, so the business is likely to be larger than for a sole trader. Profits have to be shared and so does the decision-making process. All partners of a business are subject to unlimited liability. The exception to this is a 'sleeping partner' who invests in the partnership but has no active role in running the business, and whose liability to debt

CASE STUDY

Co-op Travelcare

Travelcare is part of the Co-operative Group. Travelcare is not owned by a tour operator but is the UK's largest independent travel agent. Travelcare prides itself on being able to offer impartial advice and a wide range of holidays and impartial pricing. The travel agents in high street agencies of Travelcare are not instructed to sell the holidays of one particular tour operator. This is summed up in the 'right to know' policy launched in 1998, which is unique in the travel industry. Travelcare is based on the co-operative values of openness, honesty and responsibility.

Travelcare has 390 branches nationwide and has nearly 2000 employees. Customers can also book online and over the telephone.

The Co-operative Group is a co-operative society, not a company. It has shares but their value doesn't fluctuate and they cannot be traded. All Co-ops have members and the customers become the members. The members own and democratically control what the Co-operative Group does.

See Figure 1.9, and visit www.co-op.co.uk for more information about the history, development and philosophy of the Co-operative society.

1 **In what ways does Travelcare differ from other high street travel agencies?**

2 **Explain the ways in which Travelcare has used technology.**

Figure 1.9 Leaflets from Travelcare

Information on late bookings

We want you to be aware that on late bookings, most holiday companies make charges for the following services:

- Ticket collection at the airport
- Aviation security charge

Other optional services may also carry a charge, these include:

- Resort transfers • In-flight meals
- Increased luggage allowance
- Pre-bookable seats (Not all companies offer this facility)

Our team will give you a total cost before you make your booking!

Holiday 'bargains' aren't always worth what they appear to be. You can always rely on Travelcare to guide you through the discount confusion.

For more information, ask a member of our team at your local branch of Travelcare, (branches nationwide) or ring our national call centre on **0870 902 0057.**

www.travelcareonline.com

Offers are subject to availability and certain terms and conditions. Ask our team for full details.

Your holiday matters to us!

At Travelcare we do things differently. We all really understand just how important your holiday is, you save hard, you look forward to it and you can't wait to get away. Expectations are high - and that's why it's so important to us to make sure your holiday really is memorable, for all the right reasons!

As the UK's largest independent travel agent, we're not financially tied to any holiday company. As well as providing advice that's totally impartial and unbiased, we'll search from over 300 holiday companies to help find the holiday that's exactly right for you and compare your holiday with others, to make sure you get the very best value.

Our Promise

We will...	So you get...
Search	The widest choice
Compare holidays	The best value
Guide you	All the information you need
Be unbiased	Impartial advice
Be at your service	Personalised customer service
Keep these promises	The holiday that's right for you!

ecent research we carried out showed that:
The price of comparable holidays can vary by hundreds of pounds.
'Tricks of the trade' can mean that big holiday discounts don't always mean the best holiday prices.

artial advice to help you choose the right holiday

Summer and Winter holidays

NEVER BEATEN on price

Guaranteed Lowest Price every time!

Travelcare
21 Fish Street
Northampton
NN1 2AA
Tel 01604 626 111
ABTA No. 60849

Offers are subject to availability on selected tour operators only, certain terms and conditions apply. Ask our team for full details.

Travelcare

Call direct 0870 112 0080
Pop in to a branch or Log on www.travelcare.co.uk

Travel Money

Commission **FREE** Currency*

A Wider Range of Services
Get your holiday off to a flying start with the extra services available from your local Travelcare - ask your Travel Advisor for further details.

Transport to the Airport	Airport Parking
Car Hire	Holiday Money
Airport Hotels	Airport Lounges
Attraction Passes	Gift Vouchers

*Commission free travel money is available through participating branches only and via the website. It is subject to availability and may be withdrawn at any time. Commissions will apply to travellers' cheque and currency chosen sale.

Travelcare

Call direct 0870 112 0080
Pop in to a branch or Log on www.travelcare.co.uk

is limited to the amount of capital that person has invested. Each of the partners is bound by the actions of the others, which may cause a problem. For instance one partner might be unreliable and may cause the demise of the business, landing the other partner(s) in debt too.

Private limited companies

Any business organisation with the word 'limited' in its name implies that investors in the business (or shareholders) are liable only for the company's debts up to the amount of money they have invested.

Competition in the private sector

Business organisations operating in the commercial private sector have to compete in order to survive. Competition affects all types of business, from the market stall selling travel goods to the prestigious hotel in the neighbourhood. In order to compete, businesses must find out who their customers and clients are, and who is demanding their goods or services. They must also keep up to date with who their competitors are and how they market their products and services. Failure to keep up with trends and fashions will have severe repercussions on the business – it will lose customers and incur financial losses.

Theory into practice

Research the private sector businesses involved in travel and tourism in your locality. You might do this by looking in Yellow Pages or using www.yell.co.uk. Try to classify them under the different types of private sector businesses.

Non-commercial organisations

This section looks at the range of non-commercial organisations that are part of the travel and tourism industry. These include public and voluntary sector organisations. We shall look at how they define and meet objectives, their funding and generation of revenue, and how they meet stakeholder expectations.

Key term

A **stakeholder** is an interested party in a non-commercial organisation, such as a member of a charity or a taxpayer.

The public sector

The state (central or local government) provides travel and tourism activities and facilities in the public sector. In theory the public sector facilities exist to provide a service to the community – a service in this context means something that benefits or is useful to the members of the public in the area.

CASE STUDY

VisitBritain

The government department which oversees travel and tourism in the UK is the Department for Culture, Media and Sport (DCMS). The DCMS funds VisitBritain, whose website is www.visitbritain.com.

VisitBritain was created on 1 April 2003 to market Britain to the rest of the world and England to the British. It was formed by the merger of the British Tourist Authority and the English Tourism Council, with a mission to build the value of tourism by creating world-class destination brands and marketing campaigns. It will also build partnerships with other organisations that have a stake in British and English tourism.

VisitBritain has a range of goals:

- to promote Britain overseas as a tourist destination, generating additional tourism revenue throughout Britain and throughout the year

- to grow the value of the domestic market by encouraging UK residents to take additional and/or longer breaks in England

- to provide advice to government on matters affecting tourism and contribute to wider government objectives

- to work in partnership with the national tourist boards in England, Scotland, Wales and Northern Ireland and the regional tourist boards to build the British tourism industry and to promote an attractive image of Britain.

VisitBritain is funded by the DCMS to promote Britain overseas as a tourist destination and to lead and coordinate England marketing. The net Grant-in-Aid to promote Britain overseas for 2003/04 was £35.5 million. Additionally VisitBritain raises around £15 million in non-governmental funding from partners. The total resources available for England marketing is £14.1 million. VisitBritain operates a network of 25 offices covering 31 key markets – new markets for 2003/04 were Poland, Russia, China and Korea. VisitBritain employs 450 staff, 60 per cent of whom are employed overseas.

Why is it important that countries have national tourist boards funded by central government?

Aims of public sector travel and tourism organisations

The aims of a travel and tourism organisation in the public sector (e.g. a museum which is a visitor attraction) might be:

✱ to provide a service for the population in the surrounding area, such as a major event in the summer holidays

✱ to keep within the local authority budget and to make an adequate return on the local authority capital invested in the organisation.

✱ to provide jobs for people in the locality.

Think it over ...

Why do you think a local council provides and promotes events such as St Crispin's Fair, as illustrated in Figure 1.10?

Figure 1.10
Northampton Borough Council advertises the St Crispin Street Fair

The voluntary sector

Falling between the public sector and the private sector is the voluntary sector, which embraces all kinds of organisations, such as clubs, societies and charities. These are not controlled by the state nor do they operate solely for profit. They have been formed because of some interest or need in the community.

The aims of travel and tourism organisations in the voluntary sector could include the following broad issues:

✱ to provide facilities that are not otherwise provided

✱ to strictly observe a non-profit making rule, ensuring that any surplus income that the organisation makes goes back to its members or is invested in the organisation's future (the National Trust operates in this way)

✱ to bring to the public's attention some issue in society, such as conservation or environmental protection (e.g. Friends of the Earth and Greenpeace).

There might be some political or social aim or reason for the organisation's existence, such as to encourage sustainable tourism. An example is the charity Tourism Concern (www.tourismconcern.org.uk).

In the voluntary sector an objective may be to recruit a certain number of members per year, or to hold a number of social functions in a month, or to raise a sum of money for a specific purpose.

CASE STUDY

The National Trust (NT)

The National Trust (www.nationaltrust.org.uk) is a registered charity founded in 1895 to look after places of historic interest or natural beauty permanently for the benefit of the nation across England, Wales and Northern Ireland. It is independent of government and receives no direct state grant or subsidy for its general work. The NT is one of England's leading conservation bodies, protecting through ownership and covenants 251 223 hectares of land of special importance and 965 kilometres of outstanding coastline. The Trust is dependent on the support of its 3 million members, visitors, partners and benefactors. The NT is responsible for historic buildings dating from the Middle Ages to modern times, ancient monuments, gardens, landscape parks and farmland leased to over 1500 tenant farmers.

Figure 1.11 One of the National Trust's many properties

Over the summer of 2003 the NT gained members faster than babies were born in the UK: one recruit every 42 seconds. This record membership (3.3 million) and increase in visitor figures (13 million visitors in pay-for-entry properties and an estimated 50 million to coastline and countryside owned by the NT) reflects the need of visitors for enjoying natural attractions and visiting places of historical and cultural significance.

The price of such success is high. The assets of the NT, the buildings and estates (such as Waddesdon Manor in Buckinghamshire – see Figure 1.11), are also great liabilities. Four out of five historic properties still run at a loss because the costs of looking after them outstrip any income they generate.

1 Explain why the NT is part of the voluntary sector.
2 Which type of people do you think become members of the NT? Why do you think they join?

Voluntary organisations are extremely varied in the range of activities they cover. For example, youth organisations are formed specifically for 'young people' in order to provide them with certain facilities. There is some discrepancy over what constitutes a young person – some organisations allow teenagers (those aged between 13 and 19 years) to join, while others state that a person is still 'young' up to the age of 30!

The Youth Hostel Association (www.yha.org.uk) is a registered charity. It was founded in 1930 to 'help all, especially young people of limited means, to a greater knowledge, love and care of the countryside, particularly by providing Youth Hostels or other simple accommodation for them in their travels, and thus to promote their health, rest and education'. People of all ages (including families) can join the YHA.

Adventure organisations are not for the faint-hearted. These are for outdoor recreation in the UK and abroad. Examples are the Duke of Edinburgh's Award Scheme, Outward Bound, and Operation Raleigh.

Agencies delivering products and services

Key term

A **visitor** (or **tourist**) **attraction** can be defined as a permanently established excursion destination, a primary purpose of which is to allow public access for entertainment, interest or education, rather than being a primary retail outlet or venue for sporting, theatrical or film performances. It must be open to the public, without prior booking, for published periods each year, and should be capable of attracting day visitors or tourists as well as local residents.

There are many different types of attraction, which can be broadly split into three categories: built attractions, natural attractions, and events as attractions.

Built attractions

Built attractions can be divided into:

* leisure and theme parks
* museums and art galleries
* places of worship

* historic properties
* wildlife attractions
* visitor/heritage centres
* steam/heritage railways
* country parks
* farms
* gardens
* workplaces
* other attractions.

Theory into practice

The list below names a range of built attractions in the UK with the estimated number of visitors in 2002.

York Minster (1.6 million)
London Zoo (891 000)
The Deep (750 000)
Tate Modern (4.6 million)
Blackpool Pleasure Beach (6.2 million)
Tower of London (2 million)
Westminster Abbey (1 million)
North York Moors Railway (290 000)
Eastbourne Pier (2 million)
British Airways London Eye (4 million)
Roman Baths, Bath (850 000)
Giant's Causeway Visitor Centre (400 000)
Eden Project (1.8 million)
Cheddar Gorge Cheese Company (300 000)
British Museum (4.6 million)
Cannon Hall Open Farm (350 000)
Strathclyde Country Park (5.1 million)
Edinburgh Castle (1.1 million)
Hatton Farm Village (190 000)
The Lowry, Salford (810 000)
Glasgow Botanic Gardens (400 000),
Legoland Windsor (1.4 million)
Stonehenge (760 000)
Drayton Manor Family Theme Park (1.4 million)
Carsington Water Visitor Centre (800 000)

1 Classify the tourist attractions into the categories listed above.

2 Try to explain the differences in the number of visitors to the attractions.

3 Find out the location of each of the tourist attractions. Is there any pattern to their location?

4 Find out which attractions are free to enter and those you have to pay to get in. Does this make any difference to visitor numbers?

Figure 1.12 shows the fronts of two leaflets for very different visitor attractions. One is for Diggerland (www.diggerland.com), where children and adults can, among other things, drive a JCB. The other is for Sandringham (www.sandringhamestate.co.uk), the country retreat of Queen Elizabeth. Visit the websites to obtain further information, and then compare and contrast the products and services available at the two visitor attractions. If you prefer, carry out this activity using other contrasting attractions, possibly using leaflets that you collect.

Figure 1.12 Two very contrasting visitor attractions: Sandringham and Diggerland

Natural attractions

The range and variety of natural attractions in the UK is vast. There is beautiful coastline, rugged mountain scenery, picturesque lakes and plentiful countryside. Many of these areas are of national and international significance, such as Snowdonia, the Lake District and the Scottish Highlands and Islands.

Natural attractions are a major factor in motivating visitors to travel to an area, and

around these other tourist facilities, services and amenities will develop. For example, tourists may be attracted to Cornwall by the beauty of its beaches and inland scenery, but will want other tourism services such as accommodation, transportation and built attractions to provide a total holiday experience.

Many areas of the UK have been granted special status to help protect the environment and provide facilities for the public to enjoy. These include national parks, areas of outstanding natural beauty (AONBs) and heritage coasts.

The most dramatic and relatively wild expanses of countryside in England, Wales and Scotland have been designated as national parks. The purpose of national parks is to preserve and enhance the natural beauty of each area and promote its enjoyment by the public. In England and Wales, the National Parks and Access to the Countryside Act 1949 paved the way for the designation of areas to national park status. National parks provide some of the finest natural resources for tourism related to sport and active recreation. For example they provide many internationally important sites for climbing, mountaineering, hill walking, canoeing and caving. They are also the location of many outdoor adventure and environmental education centres.

Events as attractions

Why do events take place? Every organiser of every event will have a different answer for this question. Raising money is frequently a top priority, whether for a particular attraction, a society or a charity. Often raising the profile of an organisation is equally important. Sometimes events are organised as essentially private affairs to say 'thank you' to a specific group of people.

An example is English Heritage (www.english-heritage.org.uk) which has three branches of its organisation running events. The Special Events Unit organises events intended to entertain and educate existing members, raise revenue, and raise the profile of EH to recruit new members. The Concerts Unit organises concerts that are intended to raise both the profile of, and revenue for, EH and to provide entertainment for EH

members and for the general public. The Education Service organises a small number of events for groups within formal education that are intended to supplement and extend aspects of particular curriculum areas.

Accommodation and catering

Accommodation and catering are extremely important aspects of travel and tourism. When coming back from holiday the two most common questions asked of the holidaymaker are 'what was the accommodation like?' and 'what was the food like?' Tourists usually have high expectations of eating well. The catering component of the travel and tourism industry has grown rapidly in the UK. This is looked at in more depth in option unit 7.

Accommodation can be described as either *serviced* or *unserviced* (self-catering). In serviced accommodation, meals and housekeeping are provided. The meals provided can range from simply breakfast only to breakfast plus two main meals a day.

> **Key term**
>
> **Housekeeping** means that the guests' rooms are cleaned, beds made and towels changed.

With self-catering or unserviced accommodation there are no meals or housekeeping provided. This type of accommodation is often less expensive than the serviced type. Houses, cottages and apartments can be rented for self-catering purposes. Camping and caravanning sites have developed extensive facilities to make visitors comfortable in their stay. The sites are often luxurious, providing a whole range of facilities such as restaurants, pubs, sports and leisure centres, shops and all kinds of entertainment from play leaders for children to nightclubs. These sites are often called 'holiday parks' as they offer much more than simply a place to camp or site the caravan.

*Holiday centre*s are another form of accommodation that provide entertainment and leisure facilities. In the UK these used to be called 'holiday camps' – more information on these was given earlier in the chapter (see page 18).

Hotels are serviced accommodation ranging from luxury to basic, and from those with hundreds of bedrooms to those with a handful. A small hotel or *guest house* may be run by only one or two people, often the owners, while larger hotels employ hundreds. The standards of facilities provided by hotels vary widely too.

Visitors need an easy way of knowing the standard of facilities they can expect in a hotel. For this reason *classification systems* have been developed. In Britain classification is voluntary, so accommodation establishments can choose whether or not they wish to become classified. The AA, the English Tourism Council (ETC), now called VisitBritain, and the RAC joined together to create one overall rating scheme for hotels and guest accommodation. When you see one of the signs showing stars or diamonds, you know that the place has been visited anonymously by qualified inspectors, who all work to the same high standards. The establishment is allowed to display the classification it is given on a plaque near the entrance, and to use the classification in advertising material.

For more information about these hotel and guest accommodation ratings, contact the AA (www.theaa.co.uk), the RAC (www.rac.org.uk) or VisitBritain. A summary of the classification is shown in Figure 1.13.

Accommodation establishments can call themselves hotels, guest houses or bed & breakfasts (B&Bs). What they are called often depends on the size of the establishment and the facilities offered. Large hotels are operated by hotel groups, such as Hilton or Holiday Inn. These companies own a number of hotels and run them as a recognisable chain. However, just because hotels belong to a group does not mean they are all identical.

ratings you can trust

The VisitBritain, AA and RAC ratings are your sign of quality assurance, so you can have the confidence that your accommodation has been thoroughly checked and rated for quality before you make a booking.

HOTEL

Hotels are given a rating of from one to five Stars - the more Stars, the higher the quality and the greater the range of facilities and level of services provided.

Red stars denote an establishment within the Top 200 as graded by the AA

GOLD & SILVER

Awarded to those establishments that exceed the overall quality required for their rating.

GUEST ACCOMMODATION

Guest Accommodation, which includes guesthouses, bed and breakfasts, inns and farmhouses, is rated one to five Diamonds. Progressively higher levels of quality and customer care must be provided for each of the Diamonds.

Red diamonds denote an establishment within the Top 200 as graded by the AA

 Awarded to AA appointed establishments serving food distinctly above the standard encountered throughout most of the restaurant industry.

HOLIDAY PARK

Holiday Parks, Touring Parks and Camping Parks are also assessed using Stars. You will find progressively higher standards of quality for One Star (acceptable) to a Five Star (exceptional) park.

▶▶▶ AA equivalent grading (on a scale of 1-5).

 Awarded by the RAC to guest accommodation for excellent standards of hospitality & service.

SELF-CATERING

All properties have to meet an extensive list of minimum requirements. The more Stars, the higher the overall level of quality you can expect to find. Establishments at higher rating levels also have to meet some additional requirements for facilities.

 Awarded only to RAC accredited establishments. the RAC Dining Award recognises excellence in the overall dining experience, encompassing quality of cooking, service, ambience and comfort.

Accessibility for Serviced & Self-Catering Accommodation

Accommodation that displays one of the signs shown below are committed to accessibility. When you see one of the symbols, you can be sure that the accommodation has been thoroughly assessed against demanding criteria.

Mobility Impairment

 Level 1 – Typically suitable for a person with sufficient mobility to climb a flight of steps but would benefit from points of fixtures and fittings to aid balance.

 Level 2 – Typically suitable for a person with restricted walking ability and for those that may need to use a wheelchair some of the time.

 Level 3 – Typically suitable for a person who depends on the use of a wheelchair and transfers unaided to and from the wheelchair in a seated position.

 Level 4 – Typically suitable for a person who depends on the use of a wheelchair in a seated position. They can require personal/mechanical assistance to aid transfer (eg carer, hoist).

Hearing Impairment

 Level 2 – Recommended (Best Practice) additional requirements to meet the National Accessible Standards for guests with hearing impairment, from mild hearing loss to profoundly deaf.

Visual Impairment

 Level 2 – Recommended (Best Practice) additional requirements to meet the National Accessible Standards for visually impaired guests.

Figure 1.13 Accommodation ratings

Figure 1.14 is part of a brochure for a Holiday Inn hotel.

1 Why do you think there are different tariffs for weekdays and weekends?

2 What do you consider to be the advantages and disadvantages of the hotel's location?

3 The hotel is advertised as 'great value for business or leisure'. What facilities are particularly for business travellers? What could a leisure visitor find of interest in the area?

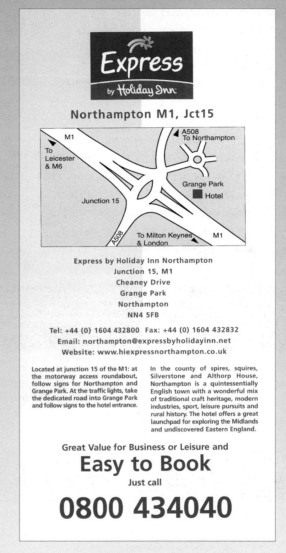

Figure 1.14 One of Holiday Inn's hotels

1 Where do visitors stay when they come to your area for business or pleasure? Where do they go to eat and drink?

2 Conduct a survey of local newspapers to find out various examples of each kind of accommodation and catering mentioned in this section.

Tourism development and promotion

Tourist destinations and attractions can be successful only if they attract enough tourists. People need to be told of a destination and encouraged to visit. Tourism promotion is concerned with making potential visitors aware of a destination and persuading them to choose to visit there rather than anywhere else.

Tourism promotion is the name given to the business of persuading tourists to visit a particular area.

Promotion is so important in tourism that most destinations have established official organisations that are responsible for encouraging people to visit them.

Local tourism development and promotion

A local Tourist Information Centre (TIC) informs you about accommodation, transportation, visitor attractions and events in the area it serves. When arriving at a holiday area, many tourists make the TIC their first stop. TICs in the UK offer a free, nationwide service. Most of them are run by the local authority. TICs can be found in a variety of locations – railway stations, airports and ports, town halls or libraries, and at major tourist attractions. TICs can be managed by the national or regional tourist board, or by the local authority. They are almost always paid for out of public funds, and you rarely have to pay for any information provided.

Most TICs provide accommodation services. The TIC will make a reservation for you at a local hotel or guest house. The TIC will check availability of accommodation in your price range and will contact the hotel or guest house to make a booking. Alternatively, the TIC may run a book-a-bed-ahead service, which is useful if you are travelling from place to place. By going to a TIC in one location, a room can be booked in the next town you are planning to visit. A small charge will be made for these services.

Theory into practice

Visit your local TIC and complete the research sheet in Figure 1.15.

LOCATION OF TIC: _____   OPENING TIMES: _____

WHAT INFORMATION IS AVAILABLE AT THE TIC?
e.g. special event product information, leaflets

WHAT PRODUCTS ARE AVAILABLE FOR SALE AT THE TIC?
e.g. guide books, maps, souvenirs, postcards

WHAT SERVICES DOES THE TIC PROVIDE?
e.g. car hire, excursions, coach, rail and theatre tickets, hotel bookings

Figure 1.15 Tourist Information Centre research

Ramsgate Costumed Walks

2004

Join our guided walks around historic Ramsgate and meet famous costumed characters from the past

HISTORY BROUGHT TO LIFE

"If there should be no human being that you can love enough, love the town in which you dwell... I love Paris and London, though I am a child of the pine woods and the beach in Ramsgate"

Vincent Van Gogh in a letter to his brother, Theo. Autumn 1876

***

"To Ramsgate we used to go frequently in the summer and I remember living in Townley House (near town), and going there by steamer."

From the manuscript of Queen Victoria's reminiscences of her early childhood. 1872

***

"Besides, my whole soul is devoted to building this church here. I have got the site and am collecting the materials. I have a delightful plan of a <u>flint</u> seaside church, and everything gives way to that"

A W N Pugin, writing to his patron, the Earl of Shrewsbury. 1846

There is no set charge for these walks as we are all volunteers but donations to help meet the cost of the walks and the upkeep of the costumes are welcome. We suggest £2 per person. All those taking part in the walks do so at their own risk. No specific liability insurance is held.

Special thanks go to Denys Le Fevre for his illustrations and to all those who have helped in so many ways, especially those providing refreshments and to Thanet District Council.

Special walks for parties can be arranged with notice. For further information contact: Tourist Information Centre on 01843 583333.

Figure 1.16 Ramsgate's guided walks

Guiding services are also part of tourism information services, as demonstrated in Figure 1.16.

Theory into practice

1 Draw a simple street map of your town centre, the centre of a town you know well, or part of the city in which you live.

2 On this, mark places of interest to the day visitor – museums, special buildings, theatres, sports or leisure facilities etc.

3 Write down instructions for a one-hour walking tour, and give details of the places of interest to be seen on the walk.

Regional tourism development and promotion

In England there are ten regional tourist boards (look back at Figure 1.6 on page 12). They are essentially membership organisations that provide a range of services for their private and public sector members. Members of a tourist board come from many areas of travel and tourism – hoteliers, restaurant owners and tourist attractions, as well as local councils, educational establishments and guest houses. Many of the regional tourist boards operate as private limited companies, so are commercial organisations.

The main responsibilities of the English regional tourist boards are to:

* have a thorough knowledge of tourism within the region, the facilities and organisations involved in the tourism industry
* advise the national board on the regional aspects of major policy issues and to supply management information
* service enquiries attributable to nationally developed promotions and to provide literature
* coordinate regional tourist information services as part of the national TIC network
* maintain close liaison with planning authorities on policies affecting tourism
* carry out a continuing domestic public relations campaign with the local authorities, the travel trade and the public within the region, with a view to ensuring that issues are understood and the regional and national objectives are known: to create awareness of the need for tourism to be managed for the benefit of residents as well as tourists
* promote tourism to the regions both from other parts of the country and from overseas.

In Wales, the Wales Tourist Board has established associated companies – North Wales Tourism, Mid Wales Tourism and Tourism South Wales.

National tourism development and promotion

The UK national tourist boards (Northern Ireland Tourist Board, Wales Tourist Board, Scottish Tourist Board and the English Tourism Council) were established in 1969 with the Development of Tourism Act.

These NTBs want to maximise the economic benefits of tourism to their particular country by stimulating the development and marketing of high-quality travel and tourism products. These national tourist boards do not get involved in the day-to-day running or tourist facilities, but set out the ways in which such organisations should operate.

Besides the four main tourist boards stated above, there are separate NTBs for the Isle of Man,

Guernsey and Jersey. All have the same broad aims:

* advising the government and public sector organisations on all matters concerning tourism
* maximising tourism's contribution to the economy by creating wealth and jobs
* enhancing the image of their countries as tourist destinations
* encouraging sustainable tourism development
* researching trends in tourism and consumer requirements.

Transportation

Air transport

Air travel is attractive because it is quick and has a great distance range. In fact, no part of the world is now more than 24 hours flying time from any other part.

Scheduled flights offer a safe, convenient, reliable and frequent method of transportation. Scheduled flights are so called because they operate regularly, according to published schedules (or timetables) that are fixed in advance. This is especially attractive to business travellers, who appreciate the speed and flexibility and the routes available, but also to leisure travellers who enjoy being able to reach their destination quickly. Ground services and terminal facilities are more advanced and sophisticated than for other forms of transportation, and so the travelling experience is enhanced. The quality of service and comfort offered on board is high. These flights operate whether or not there are enough passengers to make a profit for the airline company. Most airlines offering scheduled services are national airlines – British Airways, Air France, Qantas for example.

Charter flights are used principally to move holidaymakers on package holidays and operate only when they have been hired for a specific purpose. Sometimes charter airlines belong to tour operators (e.g. Britannia Airways is part of Thomson). Charter flights fly direct to their final destination, often at less busy times for airports (which may be inconvenient times for the traveller). The space in the aircraft is reduced in comparison with scheduled flights and only basic services are offered. Most charter flights are to holiday destinations, such as the Mediterranean, and the cost of a charter flight is usually less than a scheduled flight to the same destination as charter flights have fewer empty seats on them.

Theory into practice

Locate UK airports on a map. Research your closest airport that offers international flights.

Land transport by road or rail

Road transport is dominated by the motor car and coaches. Road transport can even offer accommodation, in the case of recreational vehicles (RVs), caravans and trailer tents.

Coaches that are chartered are again exclusive for visitor purposes, but scheduled services provide for commuters and shoppers as well as visitors. Coaches represent a relatively cheap form of transport to and around tourist destinations. Express services run between most of Britain's cities on well-equipped coaches, with toilet facilities and refreshments served.

Local bus services are also used by visitors to a town or city. In London about 20 per cent of passengers on the buses are tourists.

Journeys by motorway are faster than on other roads because they are planned for efficiency and enable drivers to travel at higher speeds. Motorways do not pass through towns, and there are no traffic lights, crossroads or roundabouts to slow down traffic.

Car hire is popular, among those travelling for business as well as leisure. Cars can be hired at one location and returned to an office of the same car hire company at another location.

Key term

Hiring a car as a pre-paid part of a holiday package is known as a **fly/drive** holiday. The car is frequently picked up at the airport at the destination.

Trains are perceived to be safe and inexpensive, and sometimes also travel through attractive scenery. Railway terminals are often in the centre of the destination, which is not always the case with airports.

The traditional train traveller is the independent holidaymaker, particularly in the VFR category, as well as the traveller with a fear of flying. Most trains offer passengers a choice of service and facilities, which may include sleeping accommodation, restaurant cars serving snacks and meals, sockets for charging mobile phones and laptops, and on-board entertainment.

Water transport

Water transport can be divided into short sea ferry transport and ocean-going cruises. Other categories of water transport also exist, such as inland waterway craft and small pleasure boats.

Ferries

Britain is linked by regular ferry services to all European countries with North Sea and channel coasts, and to Ireland. These ferry services are usually used by passengers in combination with some form of land transport such as coach, train or car that will carry them to the ferry port from their place of origin and on to their final destination after the sea crossing.

Theory into practice

Use these websites of ferry companies to discover the UK departure ports and the continental ferry ports they sail to. Plot these ports and routes on a map.

- www.brittany-ferries.co.uk
- www.condorferries.co.uk
- www.dfds.co.uk
- www.fjordline.co.uk
- www.hoverspeed.com
- www.norfolkline.com
- www.poferries.com
- www.seafrance.com
- www.speedferries.com
- www.stenaline.co.uk
- www.transmancheferries.com.

Cruise ships

For tourists on ocean-going cruise ships, it is the ship that is a major feature of the holiday. The cruise ship is their means of transport, their accommodation and the source of their meals and entertainment. The tourists may disembark at various points along the route to explore the ports and possibly sample the local fare, but they always return to the ship to spend the night.

Inland waterways

Inland waterways consist of navigable rivers and canals along which holidaymakers travel at a leisurely pace on various types of boat. They move from place to place, disembarking to explore when they wish.

The canals of the UK have their own style of boats – 'narrowboats'. These are long and narrow and often painted in bright colours. Cabin cruisers are shorter and wider boats and more often found on rivers.

The boats used for canal or river travel are usually rented by the week and can be handled by people who have no previous experience of sailing. The most popular cruising areas in the UK are the Norfolk Broads, central England and Wales, the River Thames and the Caledonian Canal.

Theory into practice

1 Get together in small groups and pick a city approximately 200 km from your home town.

2 Give each person in the group a different form of transport to investigate. Find out how frequently the service runs (if public transport); length of journey time, and cost per kilometre.

Travel agencies

Retail travel agencies are found in every high street, but also on dedicated TV channels, TV text and the Internet. All travel agencies have the main aim of selling holidays and associated products like insurance, car hire and currency exchange.

Key term

Principals is the name given to companies that a travel agent does business with, commonly tour operators, airlines, ferry, rail and car hire companies and hotel groups.

Travel agents provide information and advice to their clients. Much of the information presented to clients is by means of brochures, and the staff should possess all the necessary travel skills to interpret these. They should understand timetables, know the system of fare pricing and how to obtain tickets for all forms of transportation. Travel agents can also put together an itinerary and arrange a round-the-world tour.

The retail travel industry in the UK is dominated by national multiples. Multiples are agencies that have branches throughout the country, such as Lunn Poly and Thomas Cook. There are also independent travel agencies who do not form part of a national chain. These may be 'miniples', having a number of shops in a particular geographical location (e.g. Yorks Travel located in Northamptonshire) or just one retail outlet, perhaps providing a specialist service.

There are other travel agencies that concentrate solely on business travel. Many large commercial organisations are longstanding clients of these specialist agencies and require speed and flexibility. Business travel agencies deal almost exclusively with scheduled flights on major airlines and accommodation in large international hotel chains.

Many travel agents and tour operators are members of the Association of British Travel Agents (ABTA). Members are entitled to display the ABTA logo. Customers know they have a firm guarantee that if the travel agent or tour operator goes out of business before the customer goes on holiday, or while he or she is overseas, the special emergency fund created from travel agents' and tour operators' subscriptions to ABTA is used to provide a refund or to bring the person back to the UK at the end of the holiday. ABTA travel agents sell holidays only by tour operators who are members of ABTA.

Travel agents who wish to earn commission from sales of international airline tickets must obtain a licence from IATA, the International Air Transport Association.

Theory into practice

You should ask the permission of the retail travel agent before you carry out this activity.

Visit a local travel agency. Make rough sketches of the window, highlighting any late availability displays and special offers. Which countries or resorts are being advertised? Is the travel agency a member of ABTA or any other organisation? Is the travel agency owned by a tour operator?

Tour operators

A tour operator puts together holiday packages – by pre-booking travel with national and international carriers, chartering aircraft, organising transfers from ports and airports, buying space in all types of accommodation, devising a variety of excursions, and providing overseas representation. The tour operator then arranges all these elements in various combinations, presents them as ready-made holidays in a brochure, in newspapers and possibly on its website. The packages are offered to travel agents to sell for a commission, as well as directly to customers.

Components of a package holiday

Package holidays are made up of three components:

* accommodation
* transportation
* other travel services and ancillaries.

The accommodation component of a package can be serviced or self-catering (unserviced). Serviced accommodation is usually in a hotel that can offer a range of meal arrangements, including:

* all-inclusive
* full board (three meals a day are provided)
* half board (breakfast plus either a midday or evening meal)
* bed and breakfast
* European plan (no meals included).

Customers can usually request a certain type of room – perhaps with a sea view or a balcony – for the payment of a *supplementary charge*.

The transportation element of a package holiday can be travel by air, coach, rail, ship or self-drive car. Seventy-five per cent of all package holidays sold in the UK include air travel.

Ancillary services may include:

* the services of a representative
* transfers to and from accommodation and the point of entry
* car hire
* excursions
* equipment hire (skis, bicycles etc.)
* insurance.

Theory into practice

1 Collect a holiday brochure from each of the 'Big Four' tour operators – TUI, Thomas Cook, First Choice and MyTravel. Ensure they are for similar products (for example, all summer-sun).

2 Compare and contrast a similar holiday in each brochure.

Integration

Key term

Integration is the combination of two or more companies under the same control for mutual benefit.

A feature of tour operators is integration, which reduces competition, saves costs by reducing overheads, captures a larger market share, and pools technical or financial resources. There is also the opportunity to co-operate on research and development of new products. This can be illustrated by the case of one of the 'Big Four' operators, TUI (see Figure 1.17).

AVIATION

Britannia Airways
Thomson Flights
Thomsonfly

BRANDS – TOUR OPERATORS

Thomson Holidays
Freestyle
Just
Skytours
Crystal Holidays
Jetsave
Jersey Travel Service
Airtravel
Headway Holidays
Magic Travel Group
OSL
Simply Travel
Something Special Holidays
Spanish Harbour Holidays
Tropical Places

RETAIL TRAVEL AGENCIES

Lunn Poly
Budget Travel Shops
Callers – Pegasus
Sibbald Travel
Team Lincoln
Travel House

Figure 1.17 The world of TUI

Theory into practice

Collect a variety of newspapers and magazines, especially the weekend papers that have travel sections. Divide these up between the class. Working individually, cut out several travel or transportation-related advertisements. Classify these advertisements into those paid for by tour operators, by tourism promotion bodies and by principals. Group these together and make a classroom display of the advertisements.

Destination case study: Isle of Man

The Isle of Man (IoM) is situated in the Irish Sea, surrounded by Northern Ireland, Scotland, England and Wales. It is easily reached by sea or air, and is 33 miles long and 13 miles wide (see Figure 1.18).

The IoM is a unique self-governing kingdom – a Crown dependency. It has its own parliament, laws, traditions, culture, postage stamps, currency and language, though everyone uses the English language and all UK currencies are accepted.

The capital is Douglas, a thriving port on the east coast. It is the hub of much island activity and has a great variety of accommodation, holiday attractions and amenities such as first-class shopping, pubs and restaurants. Other popular holiday towns and resorts are Port Erin, Port St Mary, Castletown, Peel, Ramsey and Laxey, plus many rural villages. A visitor's needs can be met comfortably, from four-star hotels and idyllic country cottages, to quality B&B accommodation and self-catering apartments.

Built tourist attractions on the IoM

The IoM is rich in history; the Vikings, Celts and other peoples having left their marks on the island. These features are captured in the Manx National Heritage 'Story of Mann' (see Figure 1.19 for part of the leaflet advertising this).

The Great Laxey Wheel (known as 'Lady Isabella') celebrated its 150th anniversary in 2004. It was built to pump water from the Laxey mines, and is now the largest surviving water-wheel of its kind in the world. A climb to the top is

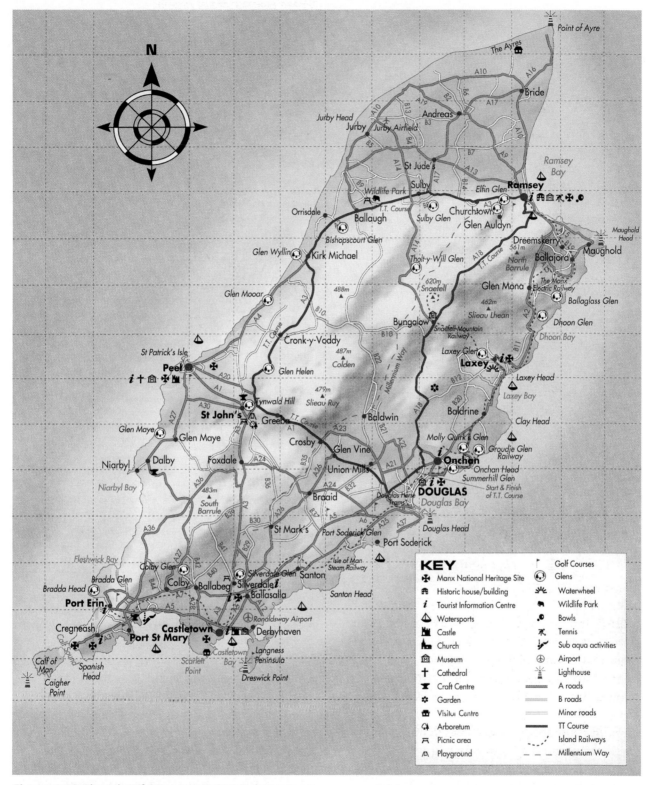

Figure 1.18 The Isle of Man

rewarded with breathtaking views across the valley. The 'Mines Trail' displays the remains of a once thriving industrial complex and offers a pleasant walk through Glen Mooar.

The Laxey Wheel has a long history of tourism. In the middle of the nineteenth century the

Figure 1.19 The Manx Museum and the house of Manannan

island's tourist industry was in its infancy, but the coming of a statutory week's holiday meant that workers from the manufacturing towns of Lancashire and Yorkshire came to Douglas and made a trip out to climb the wheel. The wives living in the miners' houses close to the wheel found it profitable to turn their front rooms into small cafés, and the road is now known as 'Ham and Egg Terrace'. The site is now managed by Manx National Heritage and National Trust.

Natural tourist attractions on the IoM

The island has 26 miles of uncrowded beaches and 100 miles of spectacular coastline. Raad ny Fiollen (Road of the Gull) is an around-the-island coastal walk with magnificent views. The walk is approximately 90 miles and has been marked by a sign incorporating the silhouette of a gull. The walk can be split into sections, as the complete route takes about four days to complete. Bayr ny Skeddan (Herring Road) is the second of the long-distance footpaths, clearly marked with a sign incorporating the herring. It is approximately 14 miles long and based on the route taken by Manx fishermen in the past as they went between Castletown and Peel.

The IoM has seventeen national glens all with their natural beauty maintained and preserved by the Forestry Department. There are no admission charges. There are two types of glen, coastal and

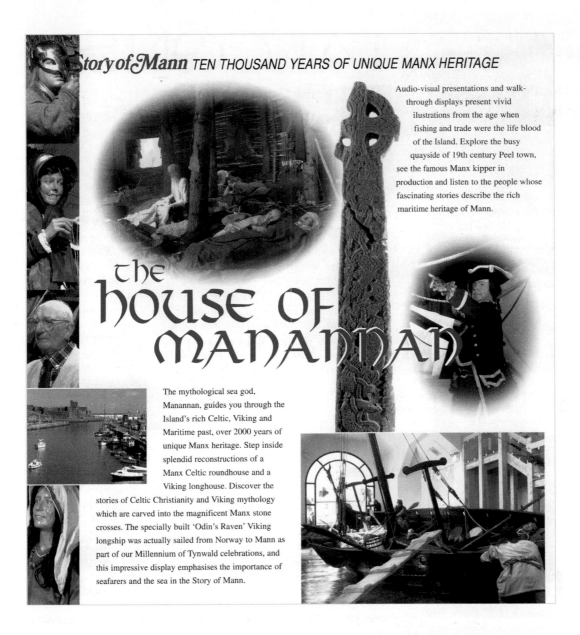

Story of Mann *TEN THOUSAND YEARS OF UNIQUE MANX HERITAGE*

Audio-visual presentations and walk-through displays present vivid ilustrations from the age when fishing and trade were the life blood of the Island. Explore the busy quayside of 19th century Peel town, see the famous Manx kipper in production and listen to the people whose fascinating stories describe the rich maritime heritage of Mann.

THE HOUSE OF MANANNAN

The mythological sea god, Manannan, guides you through the Island's rich Celtic, Viking and Maritime past, over 2000 years of unique Manx heritage. Step inside splendid reconstructions of a Manx Celtic roundhouse and a Viking longhouse. Discover the stories of Celtic Christianity and Viking mythology which are carved into the magnificent Manx stone crosses. The specially built 'Odin's Raven' Viking longship was actually sailed from Norway to Mann as part of our Millennium of Tynwald celebrations, and this impressive display emphasises the importance of seafarers and the sea in the Story of Mann.

mountain. The coastal glens often lead down to a beach, while the mountain glens are spectacular with their streams, waterfalls and pools. Many glens include picnic facilities.

IoM events

The island is known as the 'road-racing capital of the world' because it hosts some of the most exciting motor sports events on two and four wheels. Road-racing on the IoM began with the 1904 Gordon Bennett Cup Eliminating Trials comprising a hill climb, speed trials on Douglas promenade and a high-speed reliability trial over five laps of a 51-mile course. From late May through to September, road-racing frequently takes place on the island, the fastest being the legendary TT (Tourist Trophy) Festival Fortnight held in the first two weeks of June.

Accommodation and catering on the IoM

The IoM is one of the few destinations in the British Isles which operates compulsory registration of accommodation, classification and grading of all its tourist accommodation. Every year all tourist accommodation receives an independent assessment and is awarded a rating. Visitors can therefore be confident that their accommodation has been thoroughly checked and quality rated accordingly. Figure 1.20 shows an example of what is on offer.

Figure 1.20 The Falcon's Nest Hotel

FALCON'S NEST

 ★ ★   A A ★★

This family run hotel can offer you more than you might think...

There are spectacular views from many of the bedrooms, the seaward bar and restaurant. The Falcon's Nest is a friendly, traditional hotel committed to a straightforward, value-for-money policy; providing you with quality service and the opportunity to relax in comfortable surroundings. Only two minutes walk from the sheltered, sandy and idyllic Port Erin Bay – an ideal base from which to explore the sights of our magnificent island.

Superb cuisine is professionally prepared and served in the á la carte restaurant, carvery and bars – table d'hôte and children's menus are available.

All the bedrooms are ensuite, comfortable and attractively furnished, with tea and coffee making facilities, satellite TV and direct-dial phones. Baby listening and cots can be provided. Non smoking rooms available.

The hotel's lounge bar is in the true spirit of the public house. You can relax in front of a traditional open fire to enjoy the magnificent views and the local ales. The saloon bar, meanwhile, has a pool table, juke box and a lively, convivial atmosphere. The hotel also has business conference facilities and private function suites.

We look forward to making your stay an enjoyable one.

Prices per person, including VAT	High season: May – September	Low season: all other months	
Bed & breakfast	Seven days high £245.00	Seven days low £199.50	Daily £42.50

Weekend B and B special – £60.00 per couple per night – min. stay 2 nights (max. 4 nights) only available low season. Ref: AWI must be quoted when booking to ensure this price.

No single-room supplement. TT and inclusive travel prices on request. Children under 12 £5.00 B and B daily. Children 12–16 sharing £12.50 B and B daily. Reduced rates for groups. Dogs welcome. FREE transfers from Douglas sea terminal and Ronaldsway airport by prior arrangement, whenever possible. Prices correct at time of printing.

Freephone: 0500 121275 ext 2

Falcon's Nest Hotel, Port Erin, Isle of Man. IM9 6AF

Telephone: 01624 834077   Fax: 01624 835370   email: falconsnest@enterprise.net

www.falconsnesthotel.co.uk

Phone, fax or write for a free brochure and quote for your inclusive holiday. Please use BLOCK CAPITALS:

Name ....

Address ....

....

Postcode .... Tel. No. ....

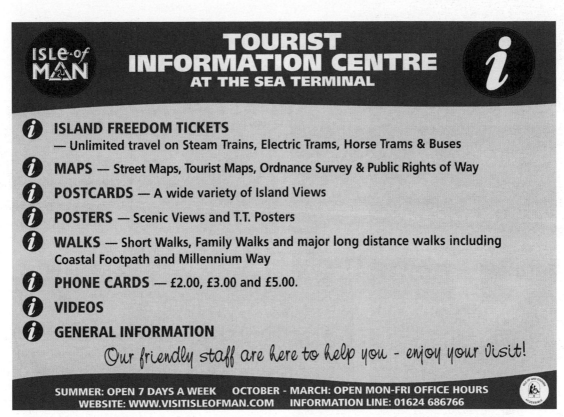

ISLE of MAN

TOURIST INFORMATION CENTRE
AT THE SEA TERMINAL

i

i **ISLAND FREEDOM TICKETS**
— Unlimited travel on Steam Trains, Electric Trams, Horse Trams & Buses

i **MAPS** — Street Maps, Tourist Maps, Ordnance Survey & Public Rights of Way

i **POSTCARDS** — A wide variety of Island Views

i **POSTERS** — Scenic Views and T.T. Posters

i **WALKS** — Short Walks, Family Walks and major long distance walks including Coastal Footpath and Millennium Way

i **PHONE CARDS** — £2.00, £3.00 and £5.00.

i **VIDEOS**

i **GENERAL INFORMATION**

Our friendly staff are here to help you - enjoy your visit!

SUMMER: OPEN 7 DAYS A WEEK   OCTOBER - MARCH: OPEN MON-FRI OFFICE HOURS
WEBSITE: WWW.VISITISLEOFMAN.COM   INFORMATION LINE: 01624 686766

Figure 1.21 Isle of Man's Tourist Information Centre

Tourism development and promotion for the IoM

The Tourist Information Centre is based at the sea terminal in Douglas and is open throughout the year (see Figure 1.21). Leaflets, books and maps, some of which are free, are available from the TIC – some have been produced also in French and German. There are other tourist information points at various places on the island.

The IoM is making a name for itself as a film location – since 1995 more than 50 feature films and TV drama series have been made on location on the island. The Isle of Man Film Commission, part of the Department of Trade and Industry, was set up to promote the island to film-makers, to whom it offers incentive packages to shoot at least part of their movie on the island. More information is available by visiting www.gov.im/dti/iomfilm.

The Department of Tourism and Leisure operates a consumer website under the name www.visitisleofman.com. The site receives between 40 and 60 thousand visits per month and provides comprehensive information on most of the island's accommodation as well as airlines and ferry details. It also contains a wealth of information on activities and special interests such as golf, walking, fishing, cycling and motor sport, to help plan programmes and itineraries.

The media strategy by the Department of Tourism and Leisure for 2004 was based on raising awareness. The colour press was used to generate extra response using three major titles – *Telegraph Magazine*, *Sunday Express Magazine* and the *Mail on Sunday's You* magazine.

Radio also featured on the schedule with a Classic FM mini-campaign which comprised airtime, a presenter promotion, website activity and advertorials in the radio station's publication.

The most exciting change to 2004's schedule was the use of TV, back on the schedule for the first time in over seven years. A 60-second commercial was produced focusing on the beauty of the IoM, brought alive through the people that live and work there. The commercial was highly targeted towards delivering brochure requests, and interactive TV has been used as the main mechanism for this. The commercial ran on a number of Sky channels targeted towards the key audience.

Isle of Man Direct

It's as easy as 1, 2, 3...

1 Choose to **travel** by air from 15 regional airports or by sea from Liverpool, Heysham, Belfast or Dublin - you can even take your own car!

2 Call your chosen accommodation from this guide and ask them to book your travel arrangements with **Isle of Man Direct Faresavers** and take advantage of our superb rates.

3 Or call us direct and we can arrange the whole package.

Travel by sea and the
Kids go FREE
if booked by 29 February 2004

Sea travel from £38 per person

Travel by sea from only £38 per person. Departures are available from Liverpool, Heysham, Belfast or Dublin. Why not take your own car on the ferry too! - prices start from £29 return.

Price Pledge - We are confident that you will find the sea prices within our brochure competitive. However, should you find sea prices offered at a lower rate **we guarantee to beat that price**. Our price pledge is only applicable at the time of booking and cannot be requested once your sailing has been confirmed.

Air travel from £85 per person

Flights are offered from 15 regional airports. Prices are constantly fluctuating so we may well be able to quote a cheaper price than offered here, so please call today for the **most competitive fares.**

Whatever you want...

Whatever your requirements may be in the Isle of Man

call 7 days a week on...

0870 889 0819 Please quote reference **XV**

or email: specials@everymann.co.uk

Our Prices include...

- Air passenger duty
- **Financial security** - we are an ABTA & ATOL bonded operator
- We can also arrange low cost **car hire** and **holiday insurance**

www.everymann.co.uk

Select '**travel information**' for travel fares

Everymann & Isle of Man Direct are trading names of **Premier Holidays Limited**.

Figure 1.22 Some package holidays to the Isle of Man

Tour operators

Some tour operators specialise in packages to the IoM. With most of these you can book direct over the telephone, by fax or through a travel agent. Most have on-line details available and produce brochures of the packages they have on offer (see Figure 1.22).

Transportation

The map and route information in Figure 1.23 show the IoM's uniquely convenient position between England, Northern Ireland, Scotland and Wales, and how well it is served by air and by sea from locations all over the British Isles. There are also connecting flights to the rest of the world.

Flights touch down at Ronaldsway Airport and ferries dock at the Douglas Sea Terminal. Flights from UK airports can take as little time as 40 minutes.

Transport by road on the island

The IoM has 688 miles of roads. Driving is on the left and road signs are in English. Cars can be transported on the ferries, or can be rented on the island.

There are frequent bus services on routes all over the island. Money-saving Explorer Tickets can be used on buses, trains and horse trams (see Figure 1.24). Coach tours of the island run throughout the summer.

The island has a remarkable Victorian transport system. The Steam Railway originated in 1873 and at 15 miles is the longest narrow-gauge steam line in the British Isles. It travels between Douglas and Port Erin.

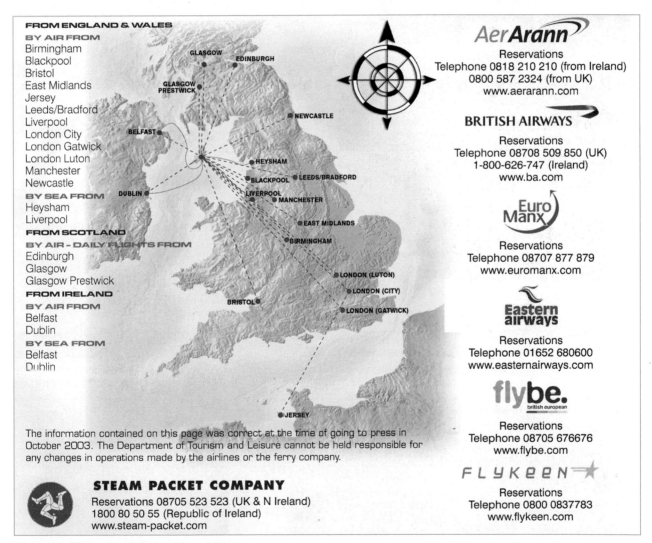

Figure 1.23 Getting to the Isle of Man

Figure 1.24 The IoM Explorer ticket

The Manx Electric Railway has been in operation since 1893 and runs for 18 miles between Douglas and Ramsey, much of the route along the coastline.

Snaefell Mountain Railway is the only electric mountain railway in the British Isles, and is a 5-mile journey from Laxey to the summit of Snaefell, up gradients as steep as 1 in 12.

Douglas horse trams date from 1876 and are the oldest in the world. They run in the summer along the 2-mile promenade at Douglas.

The Isle of Man Passenger Survey

The report of the IoM Passenger Survey contains details of various aspects of passenger traffic in 2002 and a review of some of the major trends to have emerged. The survey is conducted by staff of the Economic Affairs Division of the IoM Government Treasury, who interview departing passengers at Douglas Harbour and Ronaldsway Airport. In the survey, interviewees are classified under the various definitions of passenger type (see Figure 1.25). What follows below is a summary of the survey's findings.

The structure of passenger traffic

✱ Total scheduled passenger departures increased by 9.2 per cent on its 2001 level to stand at 673 279. Total scheduled air passenger traffic rose by 4.0 per cent on the previous year, whilst the figure for sea traffic increased by 15.9 per cent.

✱ The PVPA category (regarded as the main tourist category) rose by 16.9 per cent to 113 978, and at 117 165 the number of PVVFRs was up 17.4 per cent. Non-resident business traffic increased by 13.0 per cent to 87 536.

PASSENGER TYPE	DEFINITION
Period visitors in paid accommodation (PVPA)	Passengers visiting the IoM and staying in paid accommodation for at least one night (excluding business people)
Period visitors visiting friends and relatives (PVVFR)	Passengers visiting the IoM and staying with friends or relatives for at least one night (excluding business people)
IoM residents (RES)	IoM residents leaving the IoM
Business people (BP)	Passengers visiting the IoM for business
Day-trippers (DT)	Passengers visiting the IoM who do not spend a night on the island (excluding business people)

Figure 1.25 Classifications in the IoM Passenger Survey

✱ Resident traffic reached a new record level, rising by 5.2 per cent to 346 519.

Special events

The survey found that, within the PVPA category, the number of visitors whose arrival was connected with a special (organised) event represented 22.8 per cent of total PVPAs.

Number of bed-nights

✱ The average number of nights spent on the island by PVPAs rose from 4.8 in 2001 to 5.2 in 2002, bringing the total number of bed-nights for this category to 596 228.

✱ The average stay by PVVFRs was 6.1 nights.

✱ Of those PVPAs questioned, 58 per cent said that their trip to the island was a short break, rather than their longest or second longest holiday of the year. Of the 93 per cent who said they would be returning to the island, 66 per cent said that it would be for a short break.

Area of residence

As always, the largest number of PVPAs came from the North West of England (39.4 per cent). Other regions that provide a substantial share of this category of visitor include South East England (15.5 per cent), and the Midlands (10.1 per cent). Just 2.3 per cent of those questioned came from outside the UK/Eire.

Opinion analysis

The Passenger Survey gathers opinions from all respondents on aspects of their journey and stay. The results for 2002 continued to show that the clear majority of passengers were satisfied with the air and sea transport services to the island, with the air services generally obtaining more favourable ratings than the sea services.

A clear majority of visitors were also more than satisfied with the entertainment and facilities on the island.

Expenditure

✱ Average expenditure by PVPAs was estimated at £352 in 2002, around £68 per day.

✱ The figure for VFRs was £191, which equates to £31 per day.

✱ Estimated expenditure of business visitors in 2002 was £333, or £159 per day.

Resources

Data tables from the IPS (International Passenger Survey) and other statistics relating to travel and tourism are available from National Statistics Online, the government's web-based statistical service. The information can be found under the Transport, Travel and Tourism section of the website at www.statistics.gov.uk. There are a great number of tables and associated activities in this section. Practise your number skills using these tables, as you will find similar ones in the examination for this unit.

There are many websites referred to in this unit, but you must be familiar with Star UK (www.staruk.org.uk) and the statistics relating to travel and tourism in the UK available there.

The main source of information should be visits to travel and tourism organisations. Experiencing the industry first-hand is vitally important.

UNIT 2

Customer service in travel and tourism

Introduction

This unit will introduce you to customer service as provided by travel and tourism organisations. You will study the principles of customer service and why it is so important to the survival of these organisations, and the necessity of individuals working in travel and tourism to provide good quality customer service to meet the needs of all types of customers.

Different people have different expectations of a facility, but all want to be treated fairly, honestly and by someone who can answer their questions or deal with any problems. You will learn about these customer needs and how they can be addressed, how to undertake effective customer service through role plays and simulations. Some of you may have part-time jobs or undertake work experience to help you develop good customer service skills, and this can be valuable in developing these skills. Your assessment of this part of the unit will be through the performance of customer service to a variety of customers in a variety of ways, such as face-to-face, on the telephone or in writing.

You will also study why organisations have mission statements and customer service policies in order to ensure consistency of service by all people within the organisation. These policies will set down practices and procedures which employees should follow, but they will need to be checked regularly to ensure all staff meet the requirements and identify any training needs, and be updated where necessary. The ways in which organisations check the quality of customer service vary, but this is often done through the use of questionnaires, mystery shopper customer feedback and internal quality checks. You will undertake research into one travel and tourism organisation's practices and procedures and present an analysis of your findings after acting as a mystery shopper, then evaluate these procedures, identifying areas for improvement or development.

How you will be assessed

Your portfolio will probably be in two parts. You have to study one organisation to address Assessment Objectives 1, 3 and 4. This will be a comparison of how needs of the internal and external customers are met by one travel and tourism organisation (for AO1). You will then research and analyse the ways in which that organisation measures the effectiveness of the customer service it provides (for AO3), and extend this by evaluating the customer service provision, giving reasons for improvement. These must match the values and attitudes of that organisation (for AO4). The second part of your portfolio evidence will be your customer service performance (for AO2). This must cover at least two different types of customer and a minimum of two different situations, which will include the handling of a complaint or problem.

What you need to learn

* principles of customer service
* personal presentation
* needs of external and internal customers
* customer service skills
* assessing the quality of customer service in travel and tourism.

Principles of customer service

Why is customer service so important?

Organisations within the travel and tourism industry offer the public similar products and services, and the quality of customer care may be the deciding factor as to whether customers use one organisation or another. It is therefore important that customer service is seen by owners and managers as necessary to the survival and development of the organisation. The quality of customer service is what distinguishes one organisation from another.

The need to increase sales

Why are customers important to organisations within the travel and tourism industry? Any organisation needs to sell its product or service, and the first contact a customer has with the organisation can be the deciding factor as to whether the customer uses that product or service, or goes elsewhere to obtain it. Both commercial and non-commercial organisations share the same customer focus – the aim to provide products and services that potential customers need or want.

The positive aspects

Satisfied customers

If customers feel 'cared for' and welcome, then they are more likely to use the service or buy the product. As the products or services on offer by different organisations are somewhat similar, it is very often the quality of the customer service provided that influences potential customers, leading to customer satisfaction and increased sales. Also, a satisfied customer is more likely to recommend an organisation to friends and colleagues if a problem has been dealt with fairly and competently. Customers today expect more from organisations than just a basic product, and will stay with a particular organisation only if they feel confident in the quality of service provided.

The need for repeat business

Customer satisfaction will tend to lead to repeat business. Personal recommendations to other people may increase sales still further. This chapter will look at the real importance of excellent customer care and how this can be achieved within the organisation, so that the organisation can achieve its aims and develop working practices to meet or exceed its sales and productivity targets.

The need to attract more customers

Every organisation tries to attract new customers, in addition to repeat business, so it might want to target its products to appeal to a wide customer base or offer additional services. A hotel may offer conference facilities in addition to its core business, or it may attract other events such as receptions or be a venue for groups which meet regularly, such as members of the Rotary Club or social groups. The visitors who attend these meetings and enjoy the facilities in the hotel could easily choose to use them for their personal events such as weddings or parties. However, they will be attracted to the facility only if it provides good customer support and advice on arrangements – so it is the quality of customer service at all times which can attract more customers.

Airlines, too, are in a very competitive market, and most people make a small number of journeys by air. Airlines must offer their product at the right price in order to attract customers to fill the seats on the plane. Customers will choose the airline which offers the services to their chosen location at a fair price. But they will also choose one which can cater for their specific needs. The services provided by the airline could be the factor which persuades a customer to choose that airline over others on the same route.

A better public image

> ### Key term
>
> **Public image** is the perception customers have of an organisation.

When an organisation's public image is positive, customers have more confidence that they will be dealt with fairly. So if the organisation can improve and develop its public image so as to acquire a highly reputable status, then it should be able to increase its sales and attract customers as more people become aware of what the organisation has to offer. This is very important in an industry where there is fierce competition between organisations.

An edge over the competition

Organisations should try to provide that 'little extra service' which gives them an edge over competitors. This could be by anticipating what customers need and offering them extra services – such as the hotel which provides guest toiletries in the bathroom for those customers who have forgotten to pack them. It could be by providing transport to and from the airport free of charge, which might be important for those customers who have heavy luggage and value highly the convenience of easily accessible transport. You will often see advertisements for airport hotels which offer free car parking for up to 15 days, or provide minibus transport for clients at regular intervals to the airport departure and arrival terminals.

Happier and more efficient employees

Another feature of good customer service is that staff are usually happier working in an organisation that provides the facilities and equipment to enable them to do their jobs efficiently. The organisation should take the time to study the best working methods and include the staff in development of the systems to help them do their jobs better. It should also undertake training to ensure the best use of equipment.

If an employee feels that the services he or she provides are appreciated by both the organisation and the customers, that staff member will be better motivated to work well. If employees look happy and pleased to be working in that organisation, then they will work harder as a way of ensuring their jobs are safe and secure.

Many organisations undertake the Welcome to Excellence training programmes offered by Regional Tourist Board Partnerships Ltd as part of their staff development, and some schools and colleges incorporate the day's training package into their travel and tourism courses. It is a recognised customer service qualification within the industry. The aims of Welcome Host are set out in Figure 2.1.

What is Welcome Host?   The Benefits   Course Content   Taking Part

What is Welcome Host?

Welcome Host is a one-day training programme which concentrates on improving customer care skills. It is part of a high-profile national initiative that can help your organisation to:

- increase sales and profitability
- build repeat business
- provide higher standards of service for visitors and local residents
- enhance customer satisfaction
- reduce complaint levels
- improve staff understanding of customer value

The training is aligned to the NVQ Level 2 in Customer Service and provides valuable underpinning knowledge. (Please contact your Regional Tourist Board for more information on the NVQ qualification.)

Figure 2.1 Extract from the Welcome to Excellence website www.welcometoexcellence.co.uk

Think it over ...

Think of somewhere you have been or visited when you considered the customer service to be good. Write down why you thought it was good. What gave you that impression?

Compare your example with that of a colleague, or discuss in a group, to see whether there are any features which are similar between your examples.

The results of providing excellent customer service can be seen clearly in Figure 2.2.

Figure 2.2 Benefits of good service

Consequences of poor customer service

Think it over ...

Now that you have looked at the reasons why organisations must try to offer good customer service, think of the effects on that organisation of poor customer service. Attempt to list at least four. You may find it helps to focus on a specific organisation for this exercise.

Having thought about some of the consequences for an organisation of poor customer service, see how your list matches the ideas presented in this section.

Poor communication systems

If the customer service is poor, or if the systems of the organisation do not help staff to perform effective customer service, then the consequence could be failure of that business. If you were carrying out a web search for hotels in a particular foreign destination, and the site took a long time to load to your browser, and then was in the language of that country, you would probably not proceed with your enquiry but rather find another website that could help you better. If then you were able to locate a suitable hotel's details but could not book it on-line, you might feel even more frustrated. Poor communications would have resulted in that hotel not attracting your business, even though it might otherwise have suited your needs ideally. This is just one example of less than adequate customer support.

Unable to get information

If you ring to make initial enquiries at a tourist attraction and the voice at the other end of the line sounds bored or disinterested, to the extent that you are not able to get all the information you want, you will probably lose interest in that attraction. This will result in a lost sale, but not only that. You may well relate the story to others, meaning they will also hear the negative side and may also decide not to visit or contact that attraction. It is said that 'bad news travels fast' and, in the case of poor customer service, this is usually true.

Loss of income

Not only does an uncaring organisation lose sales, it also fails to attract new customers, leading to further loss of income. This loss of income means that the organisation is not able to carry out basic maintenance and repairs. The environment can then appear uncared for, but there is not enough revenue to pay for refurbishment. There is also no money for improved facilities, so the organisation continues to lose customers and potential income.

High staff turnover

If systems and procedures at an organisation do not perform their functions effectively, then the employees will become frustrated with them. They will lose enthusiasm for their jobs and may well decide to leave. Staff turnover can be high, which results in increased expenditure for the organisation as it has to advertise for and interview new recruits, then train them for the specific jobs. During this process, other employees may have to do more than one job, so they become frustrated too. Their job satisfaction is virtually non-existent, and this can become apparent to customers very quickly.

Fewer customers could also mean that staff are no longer required and they are made redundant. This in turn can lead to an unhappy workforce, who may be doing jobs in the organisation for which they are not properly trained or carrying out the work of two people, and therefore they are less efficient. It also means that the organisation may have difficulty recruiting staff in the future if potential employees do not feel their jobs will be secure.

Inefficient telephone systems

Some organisations set up telephone call-transfer systems whereby a caller is given various recorded options when the call is received, and asked to choose one. Some systems go even further, so that when the caller is switched to his or her first choice, the person is then given further options to respond to. It is possible to be transferred in this way several times without speaking to a customer service adviser, which can be time-consuming for the customer, and frustrating when it is found that the correct advisory service has not been reached after all this time – and the customer is often the one paying for the telephone call. So it is important that when such systems are set up with the intention of helping customers they are fully tested to ensure they really achieve what they set out to do.

Loss of customers

Customers can be fickle and move from one organisation to another easily, so unless an organisation effectively responds to customers' enquiries and needs, it is unlikely to maintain customer loyalty. This means it has to work harder to obtain new customers to replace the ones it has lost, so it is in a vicious circle without gaining any benefits.

Poor public image

The image can be affected by negative publicity. For example, if an attraction receives negative publicity as the result of an accident on one of its fun rides, or shows little consideration to local residents because of inadequate parking arrangements, then the publicity generated from complaints and possible court cases will have a negative impact for that organisation. Potential customers may read negative publicity and prefer to visit other attractions that have a more favourable public image.

News of redundancies might also affect the public image of an organisation in the travel and tourism industry. If it is having to make staff redundant, it is probably not getting enough customers. Potential new customers then start to wonder whether there might be something seriously wrong with the organisation.

Think it over ...

Have you seen any newspaper or magazine articles recently about an incident in an organisation in the travel and tourism industry? If so, what were your initial reactions? Would you still want to use that organisation? What would the organisation have to do to encourage you to visit or use it?

Lack of repeat business

There can be various outcomes of poor customer service, and organisations that fail to deliver satisfactory products or services to their customers will not achieve their aims. The outcome could be fewer customers, or lack of repeat business – customers do not come back to that organisation because they were not satisfied on a previous occasion.

Lack of customer loyalty

Customers can usually easily switch to another organisation to see whether it meets their needs better. If receiving a poor quality of service, these customers will be dissatisfied customers and they will, in turn, tell others of their experiences, which can lead to fewer customers and decreased sales.

Loss of competitive edge

If an organisation is not attracting the numbers of customers it hoped to get, then the sales of products and services will be reduced and the organisation itself will lose some of its competitive edge. Competitors may be offering new products or better services and could attract customers away. The organisation needs to be aware of what the competition is offering in order to keep its competitive edge.

Think it over ...

Consider a situation where you received poor customer service. Give reasons why you considered this to be so. What do you feel would be the effects on the organisation overall if others felt the same as you?

Personal presentation

Personal presentation is very important when dealing with any type of customer. The manner in which individuals present themselves has a direct influence on their own job satisfaction and on the future success of the organisation that employs them.

Dress code

Many organisations have a dress code for employees, or even a uniform that helps to identify employees as members of staff and makes them easily identifiable to customers.

The dress code may include restrictions on the amount of jewellery or make-up an individual can use, or acceptable hair length or style. This is very relevant within the hospitality sector of the industry where employees could be in contravention of health and safety or food standards regulations.

Some organisations provide uniforms for certain employees, such as hotel receptionists, airline crew and travel agency consultants. The use of uniforms helps to distinguish staff from customers, and also presents a 'corporate image' (see Figure 2.3). Employees will feel they belong to a caring organisation and will take pride in their work. They are usually responsible for maintaining the uniform which is provided and ensuring it is clean

Uniforms must be worn at all times whilst on duty.

Clothing must be maintained in a clean and sound condition.

Failure to comply with this is taken very seriously by the management.

More specifically:

- Long hair should be tied back.
- Make-up should be discreet and simple.
- Earrings can be worn, but no other piercing or jewellery is allowed except for religious purposes.
- Shoes should be blue or black and sturdy. For reasons of safety, high heels must not be worn.

Source: Springboard UK Customer Service training pack

Figure 2.4 Extract from a training pack

and tidy at all times. Figure 2.4 shows an extract from one organisation's approach to staff presentation.

Other organisations may not have specific uniforms but instead have dress codes for particular types of job. A conference organiser in a hotel might have to wear a dark or light suit. Such people are usually dealing with business visitors and need to represent their employer with an appropriate style of dress to convey efficiency and responsibility.

Many organisations provide employees with name badges, or a badge showing the person's role within the organisation. This helps customers to identify specific employees they might wish to praise for their customer service (through employee awards programmes), or to identify the level of seniority if raising a complaint.

Personal hygiene

People who take care with their own appearance are generally considered to take more care of their surroundings and their work. As it is often considered that 'first impressions count', it is the customer's initial contact with an individual that can affect his or her relationship with the organisation as a whole.

Figure 2.3 Presenting a corporate image

So it is considered essential that employees attend to the cleanliness of their bodies (including hair, hands and nails), making effective use of deodorants and avoiding overuse of perfume or scented products. Uniforms, if worn, should be clean at all times. Few people want to eat in a restaurant where the waiters or chef look dirty, even in the middle of a shift of duty – it could be interpreted that the kitchens are just as dirty and unhygienic. Those who smoke should also be aware that their breath and clothes can hold the smell of tobacco for some time, and many people now find this offensive.

> **✳ REMEMBER!**
>
> Personal hygiene is important and should not be overlooked in customer service situations.

Personality

An outgoing person is usually more comfortable dealing with customers, because he or she has the confidence to meet people and usually the friendly personality to accompany it. If you have a generally cheerful nature, this comes across in your attitude and voice, and customers tend to feel more reassured when dealing with someone who appears to care. If you are a quiet, shy person you might find customer service situations rather daunting at first, and you may not speak clearly enough for customers to hear.

Imagine you are on holiday and the representative who greets you at the airport is miserable, attempts little communication with customers and does not give much information on the way to the accommodation. This representative is the agent of the tour operator and your views of the tour operator could be affected immediately and you feel less confident about the rest of your holiday. But if the representative is bubbly and has a good sense of humour, you are likely to feel more assured about the rest of the arrangements for the holiday.

Personality is something that can be developed through gaining self-confidence, knowledge of the product or service you are offering, and experience of dealing with customers.

Needs of external and internal customers

It is important to appreciate that organisations have internal as well as external customers.

> **Key terms**
>
> **External customers** are those we normally consider to be 'the customers', and these are the people who buy the products or services of the organisation and come from outside the organisation itself. **Internal customers** are other employees within the organisation. They might be colleagues with whom you work closely, or other employees in a different department or in other branches. They might be regular suppliers of goods and services who deal with the organisation perhaps on a contract basis.

It is important to treat the internal customers with the same level of care that you offer to external customers. In other words, you should treat everyone, whether internal or external, as you would wish to be treated yourself. Managements usually include dealings with any type of customer within their customer care policy or mission statement. We shall be looking at these later in this chapter.

External customers

There are various types of external customer and they all have differing needs. But they all expect to have these needs recognised and dealt with, and to be treated well by members of the organisation. Of the many possible ways of categorising customers, we shall look at those used most frequently within the travel and tourism industry.

Individuals

Individuals are those customers who are making enquiries or bookings on their own behalf. They may be independent travellers who contact a variety of organisations in order to obtain information to make up their own package. They could be individuals who are travelling alone, say on business, who need to arrange transport or accommodation for themselves only. Anyone who makes a booking for one person is obviously an individual, and the needs of an individual should be considered by organisations.

A business traveller may require additional facilities in his or her accommodation, such as a telephone/modem link, wake-up calls and newspapers, express checkout facilities, and perhaps car parking.

A male traveller might not be quite as concerned about security as a female traveller, who may not wish to be in a ground floor room, may prefer to eat in a busy restaurant rather than a deserted one (or have room service), and wants a secure lock on the door of the room.

So, there are differences in expectations of individuals, even though they are classed as a single customer category. An individual customer can be of any age, who wishes to be treated as an individual, not as part of a larger group. Each individual's needs are different and each person should be considered according to the circumstances or situation, and their specific requests. The responses given must relate to these requests.

Groups

Groups of customers could be families, parties of young people going on holiday together, students on a residential break, or clubs and societies going to events for example. Their needs might include seating together on a train or in a restaurant. They will expect a discount for the size of the group, or possibly one free place for every ten people in the group booking. A class on an educational break – such as a cookery holiday – may expect to be taught as a group but treated as individuals at other times.

Dealing with groups of customers can be more difficult than dealing with individual customers, and you need to appreciate this when we look at customer service skills later in this chapter. If you are dealing with a group of customers on a guided tour, the chances are they will have come voluntarily and are eager to learn what you have to say. However, if you are dealing with irate customers whose plane is delayed, then there is obviously going to be more aggression in their attitude.

> **✱ REMEMBER!**
>
> Skills in dealing with groups are necessary within the travel and tourism industry. You will need to develop and demonstrate this ability not only in this unit but also in other units of the qualification.

> **CASE STUDY**
>
> ### London Aquarium – Employee profile
>
> 'The hardest part of being an Information Assistant within the Education Department at the Aquarium is to understand the mechanics of group interaction and behaviour. No two groups are the same, and being able to engage with the various customer types is the key to being an effective member of the team.
>
> 'Staff are trained to meet the needs of a range of customers. In terms of dealing with schoolchildren aged between 5 and 10, staff undertaking the tours in particular need to:
>
> - focus on the visual elements of the displays, shapes and colours
> - use simple language and easy-to-understand facts
> - appeal to the children's sense of danger (e.g. with food-chain examples)
> - appeal to their sense of humour (e.g. funny stories which maybe stretch the truth)!
>
> Older children up to the age of 16/17 will need a different approach. Staff will need to:
>
> - use clear signals to maintain interest and grab attention at key points of the tour
> - relay 'cool' facts about the marine life (e.g. feeding habits, mating rituals)
> - ask for opinions on more controversial issues such as marine conservation.'
>
> *Source:* Springboard UK
>
> **Consider these two client groups and analyse why the London Aquarium needs to identify different approaches to the two age groups.**

Different age groups

The groups discussed above were all of a similar age or interest, but often groups can be made up of customers of widely differing ages. This may be seen on a package holiday, where the overseas representative is welcoming new arrivals and the audience is made up of a variety of people who have just reached the destination – some may be individuals, some couples, some family groups, some young teenagers, others more elderly.

When dealing with customers in this category, it is important not to offend any age group. Speak to all in general terms, but highlight various features of the resort which might appeal to different age groups. If a venue is trying to appeal to different age groups, then there needs to be a variety of activities and facilities which would interest those age groups.

Different cultural groups

Customers can be from widely differing cultural groups, and therefore from a culture that is different from your own. They do not necessarily have to be visitors from another country. They could be visitors from within the UK who have a different cultural background from yourself. This cultural diversity can be in terms of food (Indian, Chinese or Kosher, for example), or beliefs (Hindu, Muslim, Judaism or Shinto, for example), or style and mode of dress. You need to be aware that these differences must be respected and considered. Avoid offence through inappropriate language, attitude and moral behaviour.

> ✳ REMEMBER!
>
> You will study more about cultural diversity on the A2 programme, but it is also relevant for this unit, and for unit 7 (Hospitality), particularly on the AS level programme.

Non-English speakers or those with limited understanding of English

These customers have to be considered in terms of their specific needs. If you have to give directions, for example, it is often simpler to draw a diagram that can be easily followed. The international display signage for such things as fire exits, baggage collection points or any particular facility within the organisation can be used, as these are

Figure 2.5 International signage

well-recognised and can be clearly understood. Three examples are shown in Figure 2.5.

When communicating with these customers it is also useful to try to make use of a third language you can both understand a little – possibly French or German. Alternatively, try to locate a colleague who has a wider language base than yourself. For those with limited understanding of English it may be necessary to speak very slowly and clearly, using simple words and phrases.

Many organisations produce information in a variety of languages to cater for this group of customers, or websites that can be accessed in different languages. An example can be seen on some of the newer North West trains, where signage within the carriages can be seen in Welsh, Urdu, Hindi and English to reflect the multi-ethnicity of the area. A good example to research is the ryanair.com website, where customers for whom English is not their natural language can access information from the site and make flight bookings through translated webpages (see Figure 2.6).

Figure 2.6 A website banner showing the languages available to visitors

Customers with specific needs

There are many types of specific needs that organisations should consider. Here are some examples:

* families with young children

* customers with impaired mobility (e.g. wheelchair users, those on crutches)

* those with hearing problems, including the deaf

* those with sight problems, including the blind

* the elderly

* customers with special dietary requirements (e.g. gluten free, vegetarian, kosher).

As you can see above, there is a wide variety of specific needs for organisations to consider. It may be a question of wheelchair accessibility, special rooms in hotels designed to accommodate those with impaired mobility, handrails on stairs or in toilets, avoidance of hazards which may not be noticed by those with impaired vision, assistance on transport services, baby changing rooms, and so on.

Customers with a hearing impairment can be difficult to identify as there is often no outward visible sign of their specific problem. Communication may be difficult with someone who has a speech impairment. Many organisations have hearing loop systems to aid communication with these groups of customers.

Customers with young children often require access for prams, baby changing facilities, cots in accommodation outlets, highchairs in restaurants, and lifts or moving ramps to enable access to other floors of a building.

Those with sight problems may hope to receive information in braille but this is seldom provided. However, organisations often have audio communication which can assist these customers, or braille impressions on key pads such as in lifts. Many museums provide audio guides to assist

these customers and enable them to enjoy the attraction.

People who cannot stand for long periods at an exhibition may need additional seating or rest areas. Many tourist attractions provide benches or chairs for people to rest for a while, but these are not always available for customers at all attractions or venues, particularly check-in areas at busy airports.

Organisations that provide catering need to consider dietary requirements and identify specific meal types available, or take requests at the booking stage for special needs.

Guidebooks and brochures sometimes include symbols to identify facilities suited to those with special needs, as you will see from the example in Figure 2.7. These symbols are then displayed according to the facilities provided for each attraction or facility.

The law has recently changed in relation to groups with special needs. All organisations – not just those in the travel and tourism industry – now have to comply with the Disability Discrimination Act and the most recent equal access laws (October 2004) supported by the Disability Rights Commission's Open4All campaign. Anyone who provides a service to the public needs to remove any physical barriers to ensure disabled people receive a fair service, and services had to be reasonably accessible by 1 October 2004. A Code of Practice was produced jointly by the government and the Disability Rights Commission which gave guidance on the 2004 duties and the government's proposals for regulations to underpin them.

Think it over ...

You can find out more about this through using the www.drc-gb.org or www.disability.gov.uk websites.

🏠	Historic house	🦃	Nature reserve	🛍	Shop
🏰	Castle	★	Points to note	☕	Refreshments
🏘	Other buildings	i	Contact details	🅰	Suitable for picnics
✚	Church, chapel etc	£	Admission details	👪	Facilities for families
🗼	Mill	🏃	Guided tours	🖼	Learning
🏛	Prehistoric/Roman site	🎭	Events	🐕	Dogs welcome
⬆T	Industrial heritage	🚶	Country walk	🚲	Facilities for cyclists
🐄	Farm/farm animals	♿	Access for visitors with disabilities	➜	How to find the property
❄	Garden			⇌	Railway station
🌳	Park	👁	For visually impaired visitors	P	Parking
🏔	Countryside			🔔	Licensed for civil weddings
🏖	Coast	👂	For hearing impaired visitors	T	Available for functions

Figure 2.7 Symbols used by the National Trust

Members of certain clubs and groups

Some customers are members of travel or tourism clubs. This could be an organisation such as Resort Condominiums International (RCI), a timeshare group whose members have specific priorities over non-members as regards access. Other examples are the Cycling Tourist Club (CTC) and the Caravanners' Club, whose members receive publicity related to their needs and interests. This publicity may include promotion from travel and tourism organisations and offers may be specific to members of the group. The National Trust offers special events for members only and allows reduced admission prices for members to the various facilities it manages (see Figure 2.8).

There's so much to enjoy...

Become a member of the National Trust and you'll be free to enjoy all the beautiful places in our care. Discover stunning coastline, walk through unspoilt countryside, explore magnificent country houses and be inspired by incredible gardens. And you can return as many times as you like to the places you love.

FREE entry for members

- Over 300 beautiful historic houses
- Over 200 inspirational gardens
- Over 600 miles of coastline
- Over 240,000 hectares of countryside
- Over 50 National Trust car parks

You'll receive your exclusive membership pack

You'll receive everything you need to plan great days out. That includes your free National Trust Handbook, with comprehensive information about all the places in our care. We'll also keep you up-to-date with exciting events in your area – so you can really make the most of your membership.

And if you join today, you'll get your entrance fee back

Figure 2.8 Membership details for the National Trust

Also included in this category are loyalty programmes such as Airmiles, Hilton Hotels group membership, or other frequent-user reward programmes. Customers may have preferential rates or treatment through these schemes, so obviously it is important to retain this custom through continued good customer service.

Conclusion

Having considered a wide range of customer types, you may now appreciate the vast range of customer needs which must be considered within facilities or by providers of services in order to meet the requirements or expectations of customers.

When you are undertaking simulations or role plays of customer service situations, you will need to reflect on this important section about customer needs in order to adapt your responses suitably and meet the expectations of your 'customers'. If you are in part-time employment or have been on work experience you may have dealt with a variety of customer needs, and this will give you valuable insight into dealing with various customer types.

Think it over ...

A family of four (two adults, a six-year-old child and a baby) are departing from Manchester Airport for a holiday flight within the European Union but they have limited use of the English language. Identify at least *ten* needs for this group, from arrival at the airport to departure on their flight. Exchange your list with a colleague and discuss the possible ways the airport management could meet these needs.

Internal customers

Who are the internal customers?

As you read earlier, internal customers are those who belong to the organisation, or suppliers of products and services to that organisation.

When you visit an attraction or facility, the people you see while buying tickets and then touring the attraction and using the facilities are not the only ones providing customer service. These are just the people who are 'front of house'.

More activity will be going on behind the scenes to ensure the customers' experience is a good one.

When you were thinking about the activity you have just completed above, about Manchester Airport, you probably thought mainly of things such as signs showing the check-in desk, checking-in processes, toilets with baby changing facilities, catering with seating areas, shops, visual flight departure screens, security, and so on. But far more people or services than these are involved with delivering the customer service at the airport.

Think it over ...

Think more carefully now about other services provided at Manchester Airport that are intended to help customers. List as many as you can and compare your own list with those of colleagues. Discuss the impact of one of these internal customers failing to provide the service they are contracted to provide.

There are several airline companies, baggage handlers, technical support staff, medical and emergency support staff, special assistance support and provision, HM Custom and Excise personnel, immigration, left luggage/lost and found luggage, business centre personnel, conference and banqueting providers, prayer room, telephone and meeting points. And this list is not complete.

Some of these personnel are not always dealing with customers face-to-face, but the services they provide all form part of the customer service provision of the airport itself. These are all internal customers of the airport and contribute to the provision of customer service there.

So internal customers are not only the members of staff within the organisation (in this case those directly employed by the airport) but also outside suppliers (such as shop staff, contracted check-in staff or baggage handlers, airline as well as front-of-house catering staff). They all need to work together to support the customer service provision at the airport, and there must be good working relationships between not only direct colleagues but also these other suppliers.

Threat of holiday nightmare as BA staff vote to strike

Daily Mail headline, 14 August 2004

The following is based on part of the *Daily Mail* article:

> The August bank holiday weekend looks set to become a nightmare for holidaymakers after British Airways staff voted to strike over pay. Check-in staff and baggage handlers voted in favour of action in the dispute. Heathrow, Gatwick, Birmingham, Manchester, Glasgow and Edinburgh airports will all be affected for 24 hours. It will also cause massive delays for days, with knock-on effects for other airlines. Strike action is something BA can ill afford as it struggles to get to grips with costs and fierce competition. It has already warned that a stoppage would 'seriously damage' the company and possibly put its future at risk, damaging business and its reputation.

The headline identifies a possible strike of BA staff at various airports around the country. This includes BA flight crew, check-in staff, and other BA ground staff.

1 Consider the effects of this strike for the following groups of internal customers: (a) contracted catering staff, (b) retail outlet staff at terminals, (c) baggage handlers, and (d) other airline companies flying to similar destinations.
2 Consider also the effect if the strike went ahead on the reputation of British Airways.

Dealings with colleagues

Within a smaller organisation, such as an independent travel agency, you could be working closely with colleagues. It is necessary that standards of customer service be maintained between each other. You should address a colleague as you would hope to be addressed yourself. Even if you are not happy with something or someone within the organisation, you cannot let these feelings be apparent to external customers. If one colleague does not follow through an external enquiry, you should not make any personal comments about that colleague to the customer but undertake the work yourself as efficiently as possible.

The organisation should have systems in place which enable you to do your job effectively and maintain high levels of customer satisfaction, and there should be good communication between all departments of an organisation. The operation of the organisation should appear to be smooth and trouble-free to the external customer as well as to the internal customer, if they are providers of ancillary services.

Needs of internal customers

Developing new systems

Internal customers need to be kept informed of any changes to procedures or practices operated by the organisation so that they can carry out their duties effectively. This may involve discussions with the internal customers about the current operation of systems and procedures in order to develop or improve them. If internal customers feel involved with the process they are more likely to be willing and co-operative when new systems are put into action.

Training with new systems and procedures

Employees also need to be trained to use new systems and procedures in order to enable smooth and efficient operation of these. If employees have been involved with the discussions and their views have been heard and considered, they will feel more valued by the organisation and therefore be happier in their jobs and more efficient.

Good communication between departments

There must be good communication between various departments within an organisation so that one set of internal customers is listening to another and is aware of changes or developments. So if, for example, a hotel is considering extending its conference facilities, then other departments will need to be aware of the proposals.

Think it over ...

Identify other departments of the hotel or other internal customers of the hotel who would need to be made aware of any extension of conference facilities.

Your answers to the above activity should have included other departments such as housekeeping, restaurant and catering, marketing, finance, personnel. They would all be involved at some stage with any expansion and the relevant costing and staffing needs. Other internal customers include suppliers of conference support materials, food and provisions, cleaners if these are sub-contracted, florists or other interior design contractors, to name just a few.

The external customer using the extended facilities should not be offered reduced customer service facilities because of lack of internal communication and planning. It is therefore important that all these contractors and providers be consulted at all stages of the development to ensure consistency of service to any external customer.

Involvement with other administrative departments

Some departments within an organisation may not see or come into contact with external customers at all, but they still need to consider customer needs. For example, if a tour operator is producing a new brochure, the production department will probably deal with the sales department, photographers, local representatives or agents, but not with the actual purchasers of package holidays. They still need to be aware of the types of information the customers will need to have and the overall aims of the tour operator with regard to profit margins and presentation styles. So they must always bear in mind the users of the final product in order to respond to their needs.

Departmental priorities coming before external customer needs

Departments within organisations will also have their own priorities and may tend to forget that they still need to communicate effectively within the organisation. On occasions they need to put their own priorities in a lesser position in order to respond to the needs of the whole organisation or another department.

For example, the catering department of a large hotel may have set priorities which include updating the kitchen equipment in order to improve efficiency of providing the meals service. But if they have agreed dates for this to happen without consulting the conference or accommodation section, this could occur at a very busy time in the hotel, and customers would not receive the service they expect in the restaurant.

Links must be recognised between the service provided by one department with others in the organisation in order to provide an overall experience for the external customer. A lack of awareness of the importance of external customers could lead to a 'them and us' attitude between front-line and support staff, which will have consequences for the overall viability of the organisation.

Benefits for internal customers

Internal customers may be provided with different benefits from external customers. They could receive discounts on the use of particular services, such as a gym or spa, or receive 'benefits in kind', such as free meals or overnight accommodation for reception staff on late shifts. They might also be offered incentives to improve customer service, such as 'employee of the month' awards or financial rewards in terms of bonuses or shares if the company is a public limited company (see Figure 2.9). These are incentives that are intended to lead to company loyalty.

Employees also need to have a healthy and safe environment in which to work and it is the employer's duty to provide this.

Assessment guidance

Having now considered many types of external and internal customers and their needs, it is hoped that your understanding of the area has been developed and you will be able to use this knowledge to help you produce your portfolio work to meet Assessment Objective 1, a comparison of how the needs of internal and external customers are met in your chosen travel and tourism organisation.

The Awards for Excellence

Award Categories:

■ **Employees of the Year 2004**

The Awards are open to all tourism-based businesses in the York area. Nominations can be made by employers.

Reward your employees, highlight quality and offer a chance of promoting your business not only within the community but also to potential recruits. The 8 Awards open to all staff are:

Receptionist
Housekeeping
Restaurant/Bar
Chef/Kitchen Assistant
Person Friday
Tourism Employee
Sales, Administration and Reservations
   (New this year)
Supervisor/Dept Manager

■ **Trainee of the Year Award** – open to anyone doing an NVQ in the tourism and hospitality industry – nominations are made by tutors or employer.

■ **The Customer Care Award** – is the most recent addition to the Awards and is also open to and suitable for the retail sector of tourism and hospitality.

Figure 2.9 York Tourism Awards for Excellence supported by York Hospitality Association

Theory into practice

Arrange a visit to a travel and tourism facility to meet employees. Discuss with them how the organisation meets their needs. This could be through the form of a pre-prepared questionnaire produced by the class as a whole, but used in a variety of organisations or with a variety of employees in an organisation. Compare the results from the questionnaires to identify any common trends or needs.

Customer service skills

Customers today *expect* to receive high standards of service, so it is necessary to ensure that the employees of the organisation are aware of the part they play in meeting these expected standards. There are skills involved in dealing with customers which employees need to be aware of. We will start by looking at some of these skills and how you can develop your confidence in dealing with various types of customer.

The customer may feel that his or her view is correct, but it might be necessary to explain the circumstances which make the customer realise that there are two sides to the story. How this is dealt with by the customer service personnel can influence that customer's view of the organisation and can change a dissatisfied customer into a satisfied one.

Appropriate language

✲ REMEMBER!

In their personal lives many people tend to be lazy about the type of language they use. When you are dealing with customers, remember that you are also representing your organisation or employer, so your language should be appropriate to the situation.

It is very easy to be careless about the language used, and many people can be offended by unsuitable language. The language should be appropriate for the audience. If you are speaking to a child, or someone whose first language is not English, you will probably use simple phrases and expressions. When dealing with adults, your level of language may be more involved with longer sentences. But you still want to try to ensure that what you are saying is clear and meets the needs of the situation.

The way we actually express ourselves can influence the message we are trying to convey. Try the next exercise, and you will notice how the meaning of the sentence is changed according to how certain words are emphasised.

Repeat this sentence several times: 'I did not say you stole the book.' Each time, put emphasis on the word or words underlined. As you do this, think about how this changed the meaning of the sentence.

I did not say you stole the book.
I did not say you stole the book.
I did not say you stole the book.
I did not say you stole the book.
I did not say you stole the book.
I did not say you stole the book.
I did not say you stole the book.

Get your colleagues to write down how they interpreted each of the statements above. Did they match the meanings below?

Statement	Meaning
I did not say you stole the book.	Someone else said you stole it.
I did not say you stole the book.	I firmly deny saying that.
I did not say you stole the book.	I implied you stole it.
I did not say you stole the book.	Someone else stole it.
I did not say you stole the book.	You possibly borrowed it.
I did not say you stole the book.	You stole a cheaper book.
I did not say you stole the book.	You stole something else.

You need to think carefully about how you stress words in order to make the message clear to the listener. Emphasis on the wrong word or at the wrong time can change the meaning and can lead to friction or misunderstanding between yourself and the listener.

It is also necessary to avoid being hesitant, using words such as 'like', 'um', 'you know' to fill gaps or because you cannot think of a way of expressing yourself more clearly. Often we pick up these bad habits in expression and don't always realise we are using phrases over and over again – but they can be annoying and distract the listener. It is a useful exercise to tape-record yourself talking to others, so that you can look out for expressions you should try to avoid using when communicating in a business environment.

Bad language offends many people, so it is unfortunate that some young people do not realise that the type of language they use between themselves can be very offensive to others. If you are in a front-of-house situation and are annoyed with a colleague, for example, any passing customer must not hear bad language being used. It reflects negatively on the organisation as well as yourself and can influence the experience of that customer in the organisation.

Positive body language

There are many aspects to body language, just a few of which are illustrated in Figure 2.10. For example, the way you sit, stand or walk can convey messages to other people. If a person is slouching at a desk, he or she gives the impression of being bored or not really caring about what is happening. If that person is sitting upright, looking towards the listener, then the impression given is that he or she is interested in what the speaker has to say, and will try to respond to any requests. The listener is involved in the discussion without being intrusive.

On the other hand, if someone speaking is sitting at a desk and leaning forwards with hands pointed towards the listener, this could be seen as threatening to the listener, who could react negatively to the conversation. This is almost as though the speaker is 'invading someone else's space'. This can also apply when you are standing to discuss an issue. If someone comes too close to

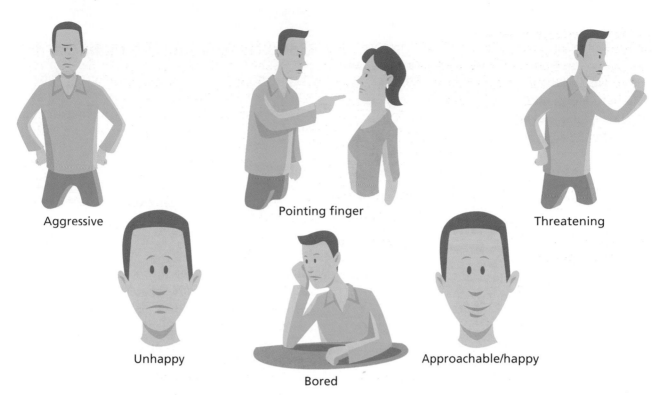

Aggressive

Pointing finger

Threatening

Unhappy

Bored

Approachable/happy

Figure 2.10 Body language dos and don'ts

you, you feel threatened and back away – your personal environment has been invaded and you feel under pressure.

Another aspect of body language which is very important is facial features. A frown usually means you don't want to be interrupted, or are angry, whereas a smile means you are contented, welcoming and approachable. Eyes can also reveal a lot about our attitude to others. Staring can appear threatening or rude, and usually comes with the frown. If you try to frown and smile at the same time, your face cannot cope with that – so if you smile, immediately your eyes become more friendly and softened.

> ### Think it over ...
>
> Look at yourself in a mirror or watch other people communicating, and note the body language they are using. What messages are they giving you, and how comfortable would you feel in their company?

Listening skills

We all think we listen to other people, but often we hear them but are not really listening to them. So much can be gathered from the tone of voice,

the way sentences are spoken, what is not actually said, and you need to develop the skill of listening carefully to the speaker.

Sometimes we are not concentrating on what another person is saying because in the back of our mind are other thoughts. This means we do not really hear the full conversation and pick up only part of a message. However, what is heard in customer service situations is very important, so you will need to develop good listening skills.

Using other senses to 'hear' the message

You need to use more of your senses than just your ears to hear the message. Use your eyes as well to spot the body language of the speaker, so that you can deal with the situation effectively. If someone is complaining to you, it is very easy to take the defensive action, but what you need to do is communicate with that person in order to establish the real reason for the complaint – then you know what action needs to be taken to try to solve the problem.

You may have other things on your mind when someone is speaking to you so you do not hear the full message, but pick up key words here and there and jump to a conclusion. If you are in a face-to-face situation, you have body language to guide you as to the intentions of the speaker, but if you are on the telephone, this is a different matter – you cannot see the body language of the speaker, so it is even more important to listen carefully to what is being said. It could be an important message that needs to be passed on to another person accurately, so you need to ensure you have got all the facts right.

When listening, bear in mind the following:

C	Calm your emotions
L	Listen actively
E	Empathise with your customers
A	Apologise/acknowledge the situation
R	Resolve the problem or refer it to a superior

While listening actively, you should ask questions to establish the concern of the customer and make sure you have all the relevant and correct facts. Rather than jumping in with your answer, decide what you need to say to answer the query, and use simple, direct language to put your point across. If you have to give an explanation, put the simplest areas first which the customer will find easiest to understand before going into a lot of detail. You must then check that the customer has understood by asking confirming questions, and then check that your explanation answers the query.

Theory into practice

An elderly couple come into a travel agency where you are the consultant. They want a holiday in a quiet resort in Europe, for a week, at a cheaper time of the year. What questions do you need to ask to ensure you provide a suitable location for their holiday?

You could act out this scenario with a colleague, completing a customer enquiry form to ensure you have all the relevant details before you start your search. You will need to establish when the person wants to travel, how far he or she wishes to travel, what method of transport is preferred, the type of accommodation required, any special needs the person has, and his or her budget. Only by listening carefully to the responses and checking you have the right information can you obtain the relevant information to meet the individual's needs.

Good clear telephone manner

How many times have you rung an organisation, where the telephonist has given the name of the firm so quickly you are not sure you have the right number? It is essential when dealing with customers on the telephone that you speak clearly and use language that is easily understood. An explanation with a lot of jargon will not often help the customer, so keep explanations simple and clear.

Clear response

Many organisations set out procedures for responding to telephone calls. These usually involve a welcoming greeting, the name of the company and the telephonist's name followed by 'Can I help you?' An example could be

Good morning/afternoon, Ultimate Travel. Hazel speaking. Can I help you?

This immediately confirms to the caller that he or she has the right number and a contact name, and that you want to help in some way. This makes the caller feel reassured. However, if your voice sounds bored or disinterested, this is immediately conveyed to the caller, who wonders whether you will give the service hoped for. If the voice is bright, cheerful and warm, then the caller will feel more confident of getting the help needed.

You should avoid eating or drinking when answering a telephone call, as this again can convey the image of an organisation that does not care about its public image.

✳ REMEMBER!

When answering the telephone, smile or put a smile in your voice. This lightens the voice and makes it sound fresh and welcoming.

Use listening skills

You will need to use your listening skills very carefully when taking telephone calls. If you do not hear something clearly, you must ask the caller to repeat the sentence so that you have appropriate information. You should also check with the caller regularly that you have heard and understood the message correctly. A good tip is always to have pen and paper to hand when answering the telephone – then you can write down the important information, such as the caller's name and telephone number, the main points of the conversation, who the caller wishes to speak to, and the date and time of the call. Many organisations use telephone message forms to assist this process, and it does save having to write things down twice (once in note form and once on the official message form). An example of a telephone message form is given in Figure 2.11.

Telephone Message

Date: _____ Time: _____

Name of caller: _____

Telephone number: _____

Message for: _____

Message: _____

_____

_____

_____

_____

_____

_____

Taken by: _____

☐ Urgent   ☐ Please ring back

Figure 2.11 A telephone message form

Careful use of language

When responding to callers, it is important that you do not use language which could be considered too informal, or slang, because this can give the impression that the organisation is so informal that it is lazy and doesn't care about its customers. Examples of this are given below:

Don't say	Say this instead
Hang on a minute	Please hold the line for a moment
OK, yeah	Yes, fine
Well, I'll see what I can do	I will do what I can
You what?	I'm sorry, could you please repeat that

Theory into practice

Create a table, putting other expressions used in the left-hand column, and what you should say in the right as in the above example.

Do not keep a caller waiting while you find an elusive colleague. Rather than keeping him or her on hold for a long time, take a message and advise the caller that you will get the colleague to ring back as soon as possible.

✳ REMEMBER!

Don't forget to ensure that the message is passed on as a priority.

It may not be as necessary to avoid informal language when you are speaking to an *internal customer*. However, that internal customer could be a manager from another department, so it is better to maintain a standard telephone technique for all calls. You may not be aware you are using slang terms or informal language, but you will need to develop your telephone skills before you undertake your assessments in customer service.

Theory into practice

Practise making and receiving telephone calls with a colleague and, if possible, tape-record your conversations. Having listened to the tape, identify the slang or informal language used, then try the same type of telephone calls again with more careful use of language.

Good written communication skills

You may be involved in communicating with customers through letters, fax, email, or memos (for internal customers) and your written communication skills are just as important as your spoken communication skills. You need to sustain the image of the organisation and respond effectively. The organisation may have a 'house style' for the production of letters, with some standard paragraphs or expressions, and you need to be aware of these and use them appropriately. It is also necessary to put yourself in the customer's shoes and think how the recipient will feel on receiving your communication.

Think what you want to say

Prepare what you want to say, and think about how you are going to write this to maintain the image of the organisation but still respond to the customer's concerns or questions. Use simple language which can convey the message clearly. Avoid long complicated sentences – these can become too wordy and the message itself is lost or open to misinterpretation. You must also avoid jargon or complicated words, and in most cases keep your response to four or five paragraphs at the most.

Preparing your letter or written communication

There are some standard techniques you need to know about. For example, if you start a letter with 'Dear Sir/Madam' then end with 'Yours faithfully', but if you start with 'Dear Mr Smith' then end with 'Yours sincerely'. The first approach is very formal and tends to be used when writing to an organisation when you don't have a contact name, possibly when writing for the first time, or wishing to register a complaint. The second approach is more informal and friendly, and tends to be used when responding to an initial letter or complaint. However, avoid being over-friendly and addressing Mr Smith as 'Dear John' – this can be seen as too personal and intrusive and many people of the older generation or those of different cultures dislike this very informal approach.

It is best to plan a letter by sorting out the information into some sort of logical order. The first section should make clear your reason for writing. The middle section can give the details and any relevant information. The final section should give some indication of what happens next, or a brief sentence to end the letter.

There are some standard phrases used in business letters, so if you become familiar with these it may help you start and end a letter appropriately. Some of these are given in Figure 2.12.

Starting letters:

Thank you for your enquiry dated 20 July 2005 regarding …

Your letter dated 20 July 2005 has been passed to this department for attention, and …

Further to the telephone conversation yesterday concerning …

With reference to the booking made by you …

Ending letters:

We look forward to hearing from you.

I will contact you again within the next few days to discuss the matter further.

Thank you for your help in this matter.

If we can be of any further help, please do not hesitate to contact us.

We look forward to receiving your reply.

Figure 2.12 Useful phrases to start and end letters

Some organisations set timescales within which letters must be responded to. If a full response cannot be given on the first occasion, it may be necessary to send an acknowledgement letter first, but this should state the time within which a fuller reply will be given. An example is given in Figure 2.13. You will note that this letter displays the sender's address and contact details, the address of the recipient, a friendly opening greeting and a heading. There are only four paragraphs, which keeps the letter concise but provides sufficient information to the customer of the actions being taken, and a named signatory is given at the end.

```
                        XYZ Trains
                        Main Station
                      HIGHTOWN HT1 2XZ
                      Tel: 0123-456789
                        29 July 2005


        Mr J Smith
        24 Andale Road
        HIGHTOWN HT2 3AB


        Dear Mr Smith

        COMMENTS RE JOURNEY ON 24 JULY 2005

        Thank you for your letter of 25 July 2005 regarding your recent rail
        journey between Manchester and Hightown.

        We regret to read that you consider we did not provide the service
        you should have received on this occasion and we are investigating
        the matter fully. When we have further information about the
        problems you experienced we will contact you again.

        You should expect to hear further from us within the next two weeks,
        when we hope that the matter can be fully explained.

        Thank you for bringing this problem to our attention and you can be
        assured that we will try to achieve a satisfactory outcome for you.


        Yours sincerely




        J Bloggs
        Regional Manager
```

Figure 2.13 A sample letter

Theory into practice

You have received a letter from Mrs A Jones about the poor service received when enquiring about booking a room for a conference at a local hotel. Draft a reply to this customer pointing out that the matter will be investigated and a reply made in detail within a week. Think carefully about how you should phrase the letter.

Compare your letter with those of others in the class to see whether you could have expressed yourself better. You could then go on to develop this with a follow-up letter explaining the circumstances and offering some sort of compensation or apology.

When communicating via email or fax, the message is usually kept fairly short and to the point, but it is still important to maintain the organisation's image and avoid the use of slang or informal phrases. There is not quite the same formality in layout for this type of communication, but it is still necessary to plan what you want to say and keep the message clear and concise.

Theory into practice

Prepare a suitable email communication which could be sent from yourself in Customer Services to a colleague in the Education Department at a local visitor attraction (e.g. Cadbury World), informing him or her that there will be a school visit in two weeks' time. The students want a presentation on customer services and a tour of the attraction.

Include details such as date, time, numbers of students and teachers, and what they want a presentation about. Don't forget to mention the tour of the attraction.

You need to make sure you include all the facts that the Education Department would need in order to organise this visit.

Selling skills

'Selling skills' is a term used whether or not you are actually selling a product. You may be offering a service to a customer, such as providing information at a Tourist Information Centre, but you are 'selling' your organisation or a service offered by your organisation. How you deal with customers is very important because it influences whether or not they accept your product or service.

If you visit a local TIC, for example to enquire about an attraction in the area, then you want as much information as someone who is purchasing an admission ticket. You need to know where the attraction is, what it offers, any other facilities or services provided at that attraction (such as wheelchair access, catering facilities), and prices. The way in which this information is given to you could be what persuades you to visit that attraction, so the employee at the TIC is to that extent 'selling' the facility to you.

Identifying reactions to persuade customers to buy

With selling skills, you need to observe the customer's reaction to any statements you make, to assess whether the customer looks fully persuaded to buy, is still considering, or is perhaps wavering as to whether to buy. Your development of these statements may act as a catalyst and finally lead to a sale.

For example, a travel agency consultant advising a customer on possible holidays needs first to get basic information as to the requirements. Then this position is developed with the use of brochures guiding the customer to possible hotels or accommodation that meets the needs. It might be necessary to describe a resort or location. First-hand knowledge of resorts can help in the persuasion process, otherwise there is usually information within the brochures that can be used to highlight features. If the consultant looks interested, gets involved in the discussion and can interpret the customer's body language appropriately, this could lead to a sale of a holiday package. If the customer looks unsure, then the consultant might need to discuss alternative locations or accommodation, without appearing to pressurise the customer.

The customer needs to feel confident in the points being made and in the accuracy of the information being given. The more useful information the consultant has, or can obtain (such as colleagues' opinions if they have visited that location), the more likely it is that the outcome is a satisfactory sale.

Theory into practice

Arrange to visit a local travel agency to observe a consultant advising a customer on a suitable holiday. Note the consultant's and customer's body language. Note the consultant's listening skills and questioning techniques. Decide whether these affected the sale of the product.

Using customer service skills effectively while selling

Skills you have read about earlier in this unit, such as communication, the use of good body language and listening skills, are all used in a selling situation. Even in a restaurant, if the waiter or waitress can describe the components of a dish or menu, that could lead to the customers being more satisfied with a meal they enjoyed, leading to repeat business.

Product knowledge

You will not be able to use your selling skills effectively unless you also have knowledge of the products you are selling. In a restaurant, the person who promotes the sweet dishes might be asked to sample all the sweets on offer so as to be able to accurately describe them to customers. This might also apply to all the main dishes too, during induction or interim employment.

A travel agent who has actually visited locations offered to customers can speak with more authority and conviction than one who has just read about them in books, or seen them on the television. This is a type of 'insider knowledge' and can be invaluable in the travel and tourism industry.

Gaining customer confidence

Customers want to feel confident in the product or service they are buying – that it is the most appropriate product or service for them. This type of information can be offered only if you have first established the customer's needs, and then identified the product from your organisation that best meets those requirements.

For example, if a customer who has to use a wheelchair wishes to book a room in a hotel with adequate facilities for the disabled, preferably on the ground floor, offering the customer a room on a higher floor would not meet the requirements, especially if the hotel did not have a lift, or there were flights of stairs on corridors that had to be negotiated. Whoever responds to that customer's

enquiry, whether on the telephone or face-to-face, needs to have the right product knowledge to respond effectively.

Use of colleagues' knowledge

If you do not know the organisation's products well yourself, then you need to be aware of who in the organisation does have that information. You can then refer any queries to them quickly and efficiently. Therefore you need to know about the roles and responsibilities of colleagues in the organisation.

Think it over …

Consider a guide in a local museum. What skills would you expect that person to have in order to make your visit an enjoyable experience? Think of customer service skills in particular, but you might want to consider personality too.

Necessary personal skills

A range of personal skills are required of those providing customer service, whether face-to-face or behind the scenes, when dealing with customers in a variety of situations. Though there is a common belief that 'the customer is always right', this is not strictly true, and often it will be necessary to use tact and diplomacy when dealing with a customer appropriately.

Self-confidence

When you are dealing with customers, they expect to find someone who appears knowledgeable and approachable. You will need to develop confidence in your ability to deal with customers. However, there is a difference between self-confidence and over-confidence.

Think it over …

What do you understand by 'self-confidence'? Try to write a definition of this and identify those in your group who appear to be self-confident. What gives you this impression?

Now describe over-confidence, and identify the differences between being self-confident and over-confident.

Self-confidence means that you give the impression you know what you are doing and why, and your body language and attitude demonstrate this. A person who is shy and retiring will not feel able to deal with all types of customers. A shy person may not speak clearly and face the customer but look down and mumble or speak so quietly the customer cannot hear. A confident approach is an important skill to develop because it relates not only to dealing with customers but also to any other situation when you are dealing with people you do not know well – such as an interview.

Over-confidence on the other hand tends to result in brash statements or exaggerating the truth and the facts. It can also lead to a customer being directed inappropriately to another colleague if you have not checked responsibilities, and this will lead to customer dissatisfaction and displeasure. The body language of an over-confident person gives the impression of boastfulness or 'I know best', and this is not appropriate particularly when dealing with a customer who is not satisfied with something. It can lead to confrontation and difficult situations which can reflect badly on the employer.

Diplomacy and sensitivity

This skill often takes some time to acquire, because it comes with experience in customer dealings. It represents the skill of dealing tactfully with situations without betraying the organisation.

If a large customer complains, for example, that the chairs are too small in the restaurant, you would not turn round and say

'Well, you should lose some weight'. You should offer to find a more comfortable seat for the customer without causing offence. Or you might offer to serve the meal in an area that has alternative seating but explain that it would be less convenient for the waiting staff. It is not a question that the customer is always right, but what you can do to help the customer be more comfortable and therefore more satisfied with the outcome.

Respect for the feelings of others

With sensitivity, one should respect the feelings of others and not say something that could upset or offend them. A holiday representative who has to convey bad news to a client should consider how best to inform the client of the situation, because this reflects on the tour operator. The representative would need to consider carefully the words to use and how to open the conversation. The use of words and tone is very important to maintain good customer relations.

Even if you do not entirely support the opinion of a customer, you must be sensitive to his or her needs and try to respond accordingly. You need to think 'If I were in that situation, how would I want to be told?'.

You need to use diplomacy and sensitivity, too, when dealing with people from other countries, as they often have different approaches to situations and different values. What is acceptable in one country is not always acceptable in another. Each nation has its own cultural principles. Although you will have an opportunity to study this more at A2 level in Cultural Tourism, everyone dealing with customers needs to be aware of different acceptable international approaches, body language and communication styles.

Effective IT skills and awareness of developments in IT

Many organisations use information technology (IT) systems to prepare documentation and keep records. An induction programme should introduce you to the systems used in the organisation employing you. Most hotels now have integrated systems, whereby a customer enquiry will lead to that customer's details being on a database for future marketing approaches.

When a booking is confirmed, this should trigger not only a room reservation but also inform housekeeping of occupancy. If the customer takes a meal in the restaurant, the details of the meal may be automatically transferred to the customer's account at reception and be added to the account (see Figure 2.14).

Information technology is used also *within* organisations. For example, paging systems are often in place to call for assistance from maintenance, security, senior management or departmental supervisors.

Some hotels near airports display flight departure and arrival timetables, similar to those displayed within the airport itself. This is a service to customers who are likely to be staying there because of the proximity to the airport. At airports and railway stations you will see examples of IT being used to display information, make announcements, and process flight and train schedules.

The latest trains used by Virgin – the Pendolino and Voyager class for example – have display panels on or by the carriage doors with details of the final destination of the train, its next station stop and the identity of the carriage for those with pre-booked seats (see Figure 2.15). Inside the carriages there are display panels over

THE CITY HOTEL

Ms Siobhan O'Reilly

Arrival: 23 October 2004 14:56
Departure: 25 October 2004 09:52
Checked in by: Karen
Checked out by: Tony

Invoice No: 10045
Date: 25 October 2004
Room No: 106
No. of persons: 1

Date	Particulars	Debit	Credit
23 October 2004	Room Charges	95.00	
23 October 2004	Restaurant	32.45	
24 October 2004	Room Charges	95.00	
24 October 2004	Room Service	12.60	
24 October 2004	Bar	9.50	
25 October 2004	Deposit (Credit Card)		–95.00
	Total	244.55	–95.00

Figure 2.14 Example of a hotel account

Figure 2.15 An electronic door panel on a train and a booking ticket

the seats to identify those that are pre-booked and for how long, and those free for other passengers to use. These systems are controlled by programmes used by the train managers and drivers and are designed for each train journey from passenger booking details.

Call centres use information technology a great deal, with redirections through the use of numbered keys on a telephone pad until you reach the department you hope will deal with your query or problem.

These are just a few examples of how information technology has developed within the travel and tourism industry. It is essential that you have effective and current IT skills so that you can cope with a variety of computer programs and systems and adapt to developing technology.

Think it over ...

Does your school or college have an automated system? If so, after how many rings is the call answered initially and how many options are you given? Do these options offer you sufficient choice to get to the person or department you want? Are there any other options you think should be offered?

Can you think of any other information technology system used within your school or college designed to help management decision-making – electronic registration, for example, automated class lists and attendance figures? You could discuss this with the Head of IT or the Bursar to give you a fuller understanding of systems used and the reasons for these.

Dealing with complaints

Every organisation aims to achieve complete customer satisfaction. In reality the likelihood of this is very remote, particularly in the travel and tourism industry where customers tend to have high expectations and the value of individual customer spending is high. Staff who deal with customers regularly on a face-to-face basis or over the telephone – such as those in direct sales, in restaurants, on hotel reception desks, at airport check-in counters – are more likely to have to deal with customer complaints from time to time.

The customer care policy will include procedures and practices to be followed in order to help staff deal effectively with customer complaints. The skills of employees need to be developed so that they can suitably pacify a complainant yet deal with the complaint appropriately, and avoid being subjected to abuse, aggression or offensive behaviour often displayed by dissatisfied customers – yet still maintain a good company image and high reputation. If the customer leaves feeling disgruntled, then that is a dissatisfied customer. If the complaint is handled effectively and discreetly, even if not fully responding to the complaints, then that customer is more likely to feel reassured and therefore more satisfied.

Key term

Complaints procedures are usually made known to the customer, so that the customer understands the types of processes to be followed and the structure for expressing dissatisfaction.

If an organisation has considered methods of dealing with customer complaints, it is demonstrating that customer satisfaction is the ultimate goal and that customer needs are important. The four most common types of complaint in the travel and tourism industry are:

* poor quality of service

* delays in receiving products and services

* being given incorrect information

* standards not meeting customer expectations.

These types of complaint lead to varying responses and remedial actions, and staff need to know how to react in any situation in order to minimise the chances of customer dissatisfaction.

Checklist for dealing with dissatisfied customers face-to-face or on the telephone

1 Listen carefully to everything the customer has to say – do not interrupt or argue.

2 Apologise in general terms for the inconvenience, to convey sympathy for the problem.

3 Inform the customer that the problem will be investigated and steps will be taken to put things right.

4 Remain calm and do not take the complaint personally. Even if the customer appears to be critical of you personally, remember that it is the organisation against which the complaint is really being made.

5 Find a solution to the problem and agree this with the customer. If this is not possible, refer the customer to a supervisor or manager, who will be able to deal with the problem.

6 Make sure that action is taken to ensure promises made to the customer are kept.

7 Record details of the complaint and what action was taken.

Source: Career Award Travel & Tourism Standard Level, Rowe, Borein, Smith

Legal considerations

You are representing your organisation when you undertake customer service, but other considerations need to be remembered. You have to be aware of various legal requirements when giving information to customers or helping customers in any way, though you are not expected at this stage to know about all the laws and all the details of these laws.

Health and Safety

* REMEMBER!

Health and safety regulations relate not just to customers but also to yourself and all your colleagues.

Care must be taken when using equipment that you are not causing a danger to anyone else. There should be no trailing wires which could trip people up. This is especially relevant if you are setting up a conference room where a power supply is needed for laptops or slide projectors. Unless the room has power cables at various points inside the room, most power points are on exterior walls and cables have to be laid to the equipment. These should be suitably covered to ensure that no one falls over them.

If liquid is spilt on tiled floors, where customers could slip, there should be suitable signs warning of the hazard.

Most organisations have a health and safety officer who would be consulted when setting up procedures to deal with issues. However, as an employee you have a *duty of care* to both customers and colleagues, and you need to be aware of health and safety legislation as it concerns you at work.

Security

This is a very important issue, particularly in the current climate of terrorist threats and violent attacks. Customers want to be reassured that their safety is foremost in the minds of the organisation. Many organisations make use of closed-circuit television (CCTV) to monitor activity in the vicinity of the business. This could be the car park

Figure 2.16 A security notice

Figure 2.17 An example of customer information

areas, access routes and nearby roadways, and possibly inside the building at strategic points. One of the duties of reception staff may be to monitor these CCTV images and be aware of intruders, so that the relevant security services can be called.

Luggage deposited by customers for safe-keeping, for example while visiting a conference or attraction, must be kept in a secure location. At some attractions, only small bags are allowed to be carried by visitors, and security staff at reception will identify any bags that must be handed over to their left luggage department (see Figure 2.16).

Some attractions and facilities use body scanners to check for dangerous objects carried on persons. Airports are an obvious example of this, but they are used at other facilities too. Though this may seem time-consuming when queuing to pass through, the majority of customers feel reassured that their safety and security is of importance to the organisation. Customers are advised about what cannot be packed in hand luggage, such as scissors or sharp instruments, flammable substances and matches, and often tour operators give advice as to what cannot be taken on board under any circumstances (see Figure 2.17).

Consumer protection legislation
Trade Descriptions Act 1968
When you are giving information to consumers you need to be aware of the Trade Descriptions Act, which requires that information be accurate and reliable. This means that organisations cannot state something as being a fact when it is not accurate. A good example is a hotel that advertises itself as being 'five minutes from the beach' – is that five minutes on foot, or by car? It would be safer to give the actual distance to the beach so that the potential customer has a more accurate impression. So, when you are describing facilities to a customer, the description must be as accurate as possible.

Consumer Credit Act 1974
Another form of consumer protection is given by the Consumer Credit Act. If you are responsible for taking payments from customers you need to be aware of the regulations which relate to payment by credit or debit card, and the need to

check the customer's details carefully when processing payments. Customers should also be informed if there are additional charges made by the organisation for payment by credit card, in case they prefer to pay by another method. Some organisations add a percentage (say one or two per cent) to payments made by credit card.

EU Directive on Package Travel 1995

The EU Package Travel Directive may affect dealings with customers, especially if you are working within a travel agency or for a tour operator. The components that make up a holiday package should be provided as described originally to the customer at the time of booking. So, for example, if transfers are included in the price then they should be made available to the holidaymaker.

✱ REMEMBER!

Although you do not need to study all the finer details of the relevant legislation, you do need to be aware of these issues when dealing with customers and apply them in your role play or simulation exercises.

Theory into practice

Study the brochures of various tour operators and identify several situations where legal requirements have been considered. You may find it useful to look also at the section on 'booking conditions' at the back or front of many brochures to identify legislation or regulations that are in place to protect the operator and the consumer.

Assessment guidance

You will have to undertake activities involving customer service situations for your assessment, and these should be as realistic as possible. Whether you are an extrovert or an introvert, you need to *convey* a happy, confident image, performing to a reasonable standard in order to achieve good marks for the practical performance of customer service. Remember all the pointers you have been given about communication, body language and personal skills. Practise these as often as you can.

Assessing the quality of customer service

Because organisations in the travel and tourism industry offer products and services that are similar to those of their competitors, they need to continually monitor and assess their provision of customer service. This will also help them to set and maintain standards of customer service, and to identify areas where it could be improved in order to exceed their customers' needs and expectations. Various methods are used to assess the current provision of customer service and we shall be looking at some of these.

Before it can set out customer service practices and procedures, an organisation needs to identify clearly its *aims* and *objectives*. This might be in the form of a 'mission statement'.

Mission statements

The use of mission statements (or customer charters) has increased in recent times, following government initiatives to promote customer service. They set out the main aims of the organisation to the public and its staff. Other organisations may have a strategy which is not necessarily written down but can be summed up by simple statements of objectives. The staff employed by the organisation are therefore aware of what they are working towards, and the public may be influenced to use that organisation. Some examples of mission statements or strategies of well-known travel and tourism organisations are set out in this section.

A mission or vision statement may be quite brief, but it should be clear, be easily understood by employees, reflect the values, beliefs, philosophies and culture of the organisation, and be broad enough to allow flexibility. Two examples are given below:

The Ritz–Carlton is a place where the genuine care and comfort of our guests is our highest mission

[Ritz–Carlton]

Exceptional service from exceptional people

[Thomas Cook]

A charter, on the other hand, may express broader aims and intentions of the organisation but should still emphasise the main issues that the organisation can monitor and control. Three examples are given below:

We take your comfort and safety very seriously. We want you to be able to relax, enjoy yourself and get to your destination on time and unruffled. Our staff are trained to look after your every need – be sure to ask them if you need any help, or have any comments. The National Rail Conditions of Carriage sets out the service standards that all train companies must meet and also explains the legal contract you have with us when you buy a ticket and travel. You can pick up a copy of this leaflet at any ticket office. Our charter builds upon those standards. It explains clearly the high performance standards we have set ourselves, and how we will make it up to you if things go wrong. In many cases, we are more generous than we are required to be under the National Rail Conditions of Carriage.

[GNER Passenger's Charter:
www.gner.co.uk/pages/pcharter/html]

Saga is committed to providing the highest standards of service from the moment you book direct with us, right through every aspect of your holiday. We take care of all the details, leaving you free to relax and enjoy yourself on your well-earned holiday. Saga has more than 50 years' experience of organising holidays for discerning travellers. We believe our success is based on our personal service, attention to detail and our continual response to the suggestions of our holidaymakers.

[Saga Holidays: Winter Escapes brochure 2004–2005]

As a company – profitability will be achieved through quality investment and training, excellent relationship marketing and a unique commitment to service.

As a hotel – we will be the best and most successful hotel in Wales and the South West of England, customer driven and delivering constant service and value.

As an employer – we will be an employer of excellence, who invests in its people.

As a neighbour – we will be active within our local community and the wider community of Cardiff and Wales

[St David's Hotel and Spa, Cardiff: RF Hotels,
www.springboarduk.org.uk]

Quality criteria

Having set out the mission statement and standards the organisation is working towards, it needs then to set out the *quality criteria* to help it achieve these aims. If the quality criteria are clearly laid out, then it is possible for the performance of the organisation to be assessed against them. The quality criteria usually used by travel and tourism organisations are discussed below.

Price or value for money

Most customers are concerned with the price they pay for goods and services, so organisations consider the price they are charging and how this compares with other providers of similar services. You may have seen features in national newspapers, for example, which compare various theme parks in the UK for price and value for money. These articles will have covered the range of rides or attractions available at the theme park and the prices charged, either for each ride or for a day ticket. Customers can then study the article and consider the views expressed in order to form judgements as to whether X park is cheaper than Y park. But if customers consider that the price charged at Y park offers better *value for money* than that for X park, they may be more persuaded to visit that park.

So when an organisation is setting its prices it needs to consider not only what price the competition is offering, but what other features may be included in that price to give the impression of better value to the customer.

Consistency and accuracy

Is the customer service provided by the organisation consistent? Is there the same quality provided whoever is on duty, in all departments, at all times? It may be excellent at reception, for example, in a hotel, but the restaurant is not providing excellent customer service which matches reception. Or a customer making an enquiry at a travel agency may find that one of the consultants works hard to meet the customer's needs whereas another takes a more laid-back approach and does not ask the appropriate questions to really ascertain the needs of the customer. The quality of service is not consistent between these two employees and there is obviously a need for training to ensure that this provision is more reliable and uniform.

Accuracy also needs to be monitored to ensure that information produced or provided by the organisation is always appropriate. If you receive inaccurate travel details for a planned journey, that will frustrate you and make you feel that the organisation providing the information is not 'on the ball'. You might even miss your flight or connections! So there needs to be some section in the measurement of quality criteria that considers accuracy of detail.

Reliability

If something is promised to a customer, is that promise kept or a good reason given for it not being fulfilled? A customer asking for a morning wake-up call at 6.30 is not going to be very pleased, particularly if there is a plane to catch, if that call does not come through until 6.45. A train arriving late causes problems for those with on-going connections to catch or those needing to attend a meeting at a set time. A visit to a theme park will be disappointing if one of the main rides the customer wishes to visit has broken down and no notification was given at the ticket office or anywhere else on the park.

Quality of service should aim to provide a reliable service at all times. Organisations aim to meet the customers' expectations in terms of reliability, but this needs to be checked frequently to assess whether these expectations are being met.

Staffing levels

No one likes to be kept waiting longer than necessary, so organisations need to consider the levels of staffing required at different times of the day, and possibly at different periods in the year. An attraction that is very seasonal may require the majority of the staff only during the main operating period, but there might be a need for some staffing at other times to maintain a minimum service.

The Tourism Office in Blackpool, for instance, requires maximum staffing during the main holiday season. But Blackpool has attractions that are open all through the year, and there is also demand from conference delegates and other events arranged during the quieter months, as well as people making enquiries about the next holiday season. So the varying staffing level needs to be considered in order to avoid excessive delays in providing information.

Extra staff may need to be employed at peak times for many facilities, so each organisation needs to be aware of when the peak times are (whether during a day or on certain occasions during the year) in order to meet customer's expectations of quick, efficient service.

Staffing qualities

If an organisation has to employ seasonal staff or extra staff for peak periods, it is just as important for these people to be trained in the customer service practices of that organisation, so that the customer does not experience a reduced quality of service because the employee is 'only temporary'.

Many major events employ casual staff for the period of the event only (perhaps for two or three days), but these people must deliver the same quality of customer service as permanent employees. Consider some major sporting events, such as the Grand National at Aintree and the Wimbledon tennis championships. Obviously the organisers will need a fair number of casual staff to provide services and products during these events. These people will often be employed only for the short duration of the event, but they will need to be selected according to their ability to provide a service consistent with the aims of the event. Their period of employment usually includes some time before the event to undergo customer service training and induction into the accepted practices to be followed.

Enjoyment of the experience

Whether you are visiting a theme park, going on holiday, travelling on business, or attending a sporting event, the experience you have should be as enjoyable as possible. If you come away unhappy, you are unlikely to repeat the experience. Therefore, organisations in the travel and tourism industry need to check that they are providing the quality of experience the customer expects so that they can hope to receive repeat business and increased sales.

> ### Think it over ...
>
> Think of a recent enjoyable activity related to travel and tourism you have undertaken. What made the experience enjoyable? Was it the service you received? Was it because you considered it to be value for money? Why might this activity have been more enjoyable than others you have been involved with? If you were asked to write an evaluation of the experience to the organisation providing the activity, what would be the main points you choose to praise in your letter?

Health and safety

Customers want to feel sure that their health and safety has been considered properly, so organisations need to monitor the maintenance of facilities and equipment. While they have a duty of care to all customers as a legal requirement, many organisations will undertake regular checks to ensure that they not only meet the minimum requirements of the legislation but also put into place additional procedures to avoid complaints about health and safety issues.

Obviously, all forms of transport need to meet the minimum standards of safety required by passengers, but sometimes extra actions are taken to ensure passenger safety. For example, some long-distance train services can become overcrowded, such as the one from Plymouth to Glasgow with peak passenger loading usually in the part of the journey from Birmingham to Scotland. The train manager will request passengers to make sure that their luggage is stored safely in the overhead compartments provided. If the service is exceptionally busy and there are many standing passengers with unstowed luggage, it might be necessary to close the on-board shop because it would be unsafe for passengers to carry hot drinks and food down the aisles and through lobbies.

> ### ✳ REMEMBER!
>
> Employees need to know what actions they must take to ensure the health and safety of customers at all times.

> ### Think it over ...
>
> Have you seen signs warning of dangers or hazards at a venue? Why does the organisation display these? What other health and safety actions have you noticed at venues?

Cleanliness and hygiene

The appearance of premises or facilities, both inside and out, can affect how customers feel about the organisation. If these are clean, then customers get the impression the organisation cares about its environment – and if it cares about the environment it probably cares about its customers. If the area looks dirty or untidy then this is likely to create the opposite impression – that the organisation is uncaring of the customer experience. First impressions count when considering customers' expectations, and the appearance of staff and facilities does affect judgements made.

Hygiene is also important, particularly where food is being served or prepared. The presence of staff with dirty hands and nails or poor personal hygiene will affect customers' decisions, so many organisations set out practices and procedures for all staff to follow to try to maintain good customer relations.

To help the overall appearance of the environment, some train companies now employ people to clear away rubbish and litter from carriages to keep areas tidy and avoid problems that may affect health and safety. Catering companies often have signs in toilets and the kitchen to remind staff to wash hands regularly – they cannot afford to get a bad reputation through food poisoning or poor hygiene practices.

Accessibility and availability of products and services

Is the product or service available?

Nothing is more annoying than visiting a supermarket for a certain product only to find a notice saying 'Sorry, temporarily out of stock'. If you visit a travel agency, you expect to be able to access brochures from a range of companies for a wide variety of holidays in order to make an informed choice. When the brochures are not available for you to browse through, your reaction may be to try another agency, and if their shelves are more fully stocked it may persuade you to use that agency for your booking.

How broad is the access to the product or service?

Many organisations make their products more accessible by offering them through a range of media – on-line, direct sell, mail order or through intermediaries such as Tourist Information Centres.

Accessibility of products and services relates to how the customer can access them and the wider choice they have can influence their decisions. This can include opening times of an organisation – many travel agencies now open on Sundays to attract those customers who are not able to make bookings during normal business hours.

Is the product or service physically accessible?

Another aspect of accessibility is actual physical access to the products and services, especially for those who are not fully mobile. Can the customer reach the product on the shelves? Can the customer get into the premises – through the doors, up steps or stairs? These aspects are just as important when assessing the quality of customer service – a competitor may have better access and will therefore attract certain customers.

Where exactly is the product or service?

Can the customer find the facility? This is another aspect of access and availability that affects choice. Most tourist attractions now provide locational maps on their publicity, but there are often also signs on major routes directing customers to attractions. The easier it is to locate a facility, the more visitors it is likely to receive.

Is there a wide enough choice to suit different needs?

We have already seen that customers have a range of different needs, so the organisation must consider how these are to be met. Does it offer a variety of services or products to suit a variety of customers, or is its market so restricted that it will appeal only to one type of customer? This could limit the potential earnings of the organisation. Though an attraction may be targeted at a specific group, such as children, these are usually accompanied by adults. So the organisation must consider the needs of the adults as well and provide facilities and services to suit.

Theory into practice

Undertake a survey of travel agencies in your area. Consider accessibility of the brochures, physical access to the premises and space inside, location of the facility, and choice of brochures. Compare the features of the different agencies, then visit the web pages of the travel agencies to discover whether products are available through other media.

Customer care policies

A customer care policy sets out guidelines concerning the most effective ways of dealing with customers within the organisation. This policy is likely to be introduced to new employees during an induction programme, to ensure that all employees within the organisation understand the relevance of the policy and how it applies to them when dealing with customers in a range of situations.

It sets out the practices and procedures that employees should follow when dealing with customers in order to maintain a standard of performance for all. It can also lead to identification of training needs if an employee is not meeting those standards at all times. An example of a customer service policy is given in Figure 2.18.

- A good range of product knowledge

- Friendly and helpful staff

- Well-presented and appropriately dressed staff

- A diverse range of information to ensure that all customers are completely satisfied when they visit the TIC

- Prompt service when dealing with written, telephone and oral communications

- Adequate supplies of promotional materials displayed and available at all times

---

Figure 2.18 Key customer service quality criteria for a Tourist Information Centre

Monitoring the provision of customer service

In order to establish how well the organisation is meeting the needs of its customers and its customer service policy, it must undertake regular *quality checks* and obtain *feedback* from customers. It can remain competitive only if it is actually providing what the customer wants.

You need to be aware of the many ways in which this analysis can be undertaken, and the reasons for their usage. Some of the techniques are informal, others are more formal. Some are quality checks undertaken internally, others involve customers both internal and external. The findings should be fully considered by management in order to develop the quality of customer service.

Informal feedback

This can take the form of simple questions, preferably requiring little more than a standard 'Yes' or 'No' answer – even these simple answers can lead to development. For example, if you are dining in a restaurant and the head waiter comes to ask whether everything is satisfactory, or if you are enjoying your meal, this is not just being polite. It is a form of feedback. This is the time not only to comment on good or superb service or food, but also to identify anything that could be improved. The head waiter can note any relevant comments and discuss them with the management. If the comments seem valid they could lead to improved service.

Other informal feedback can come from the staff. They may identify a problem or an area that could be improved. Some organisations offer rewards for staff who suggest a positive development that is then taken up within the organisation. It could be something as simple as the order in which a buffet is laid out, or a physical change to the working area that improves the service given to customers.

Management may discuss issues not only with heads of department, but also with employees, as a way of checking that the service they provide meets the needs of customers. If this is done informally, employees do not feel threatened by the situation and may be more honest with their comments.

Suppliers may also be asked for feedback on the organisation's systems or procedures. They can also be forewarned of extra demand, such as when the organisation is aware of a probable increased demand for a product because of a special promotion. The suppliers will need to know so that they can ensure stocks are available. An exhibitor at a trade fair will want sufficient copies of brochures and publicity material, but may warn the suppliers that extra material may be needed if demand exceeds that anticipated.

Surveys

These might be face-to-face surveys with pre-prepared questions that can then be analysed. Alternatively, they might be pro formas left at venues for participants to complete. Most tour operators issue customers with pro forma survey forms to be completed, often with a prize or reward offered to encourage participation. These are designed to give immediate feedback to the operator on the services provided, the support from the operator, and the accommodation or location. These are also often used to obtain additional information about the customer in order to develop a profile of customers, to group them according to age, income, family size etc. which may be used in future marketing campaigns.

Part of a survey form from Cresta Holidays is shown in Figure 2.19. This was sent to customers with their tickets for the holiday they had booked. The postage for the form was prepaid so as not to discourage responses, and a voucher for money off a new booking was on offer.

Other organisations have simpler feedback survey forms for customers to complete, such as the one in Figure 2.20

A £20 THANK YOU FROM **CRESTA**

Firstly, I'd like to thank you for choosing Cresta. At Cresta we value service above all else and we would like your opinions on how we did so we can further improve our holidays for the future.

Please use this feedback form, when you return from holiday to tell us about you and how your trip went.
Please complete before returning the form to us by FREEPOST.
Thank you again, on the receipt of a completed feedback form, we will send you a voucher worth up to £20 off your next booking with Cresta, please allow 28 days for delivery of your voucher from the day you post the questionnaire.

Thanks again,

Steve Kimber

Steve Kimber
Managing Director

One voucher per booking
Please write clearly using BLUE or BLACK ink in CAPITAL LETTERS

YOUR CRESTA HOLIDAY

1 Your booking Reference: ....

2 Which Cresta brochure did you book from?
☐ Cities ☐ Choices ☐ France
☐ Italy ☐ Golf ☐ Paris & Amsterdam
☐ Ireland ☐ Disney ☐ Worldwide
☐ Eurostar ☐ Spain & Portugal

3
a How did your party travel?
☐ Fly ☐ Eurotunnel
☐ Eurostar ☐ Ferry

b Did you book car hire with us?
☐ Yes ☐ No

4
a Which country(s) did you visit?
i) ....
ii) ....
iii) ....

b Which City/resort(s) did you stay in?
i) ....
ii) ....
iii) ....

c Which accommodation(s) did you stay in?
i) ....
ii) ....
iii) ....

5
a How long prior to departure was your holiday booked
☐ Within 1 month ☐ 1-3 months
☐ 4-6 months ☐ 7 months or more

b What was your date of departure from the UK?
☐☐ D ☐☐ M ☐☐☐☐ Y

c How many nights did you stay for? (Please circle)
1 2 3 4 5 6 7 8+

6
a How many adults in your party? (Please circle)
1 2 3 4 5 6 7 8+

b How many children (3-16)? (Please circle)
1 2 3 4 5 6+

c How many infants (2 or under)? (Please circle)
1 2 3 4 5 6+

Figure 2.19 A customer feedback form

ASTON BUSINESS SCHOOL

MANAGEMENT DEVELOPMENT CENTRE

We Value Your Opinion

We hope you had an enjoyable and successful event with us here at the Management Development Centre. We are dedicated to continuous improvement and would appreciate your help in filling in this quick questionnaire to evaluate the service we offer to our customers. Please rate the following questions and feel free to make any additional comments at the bottom. Thank you for taking the time to help us help you. (1=Poor 2=Fair 3=Good 4=Excellent)

	1	2	3	4
Was the Management Development Centre easy to find?	☐	☐	☐	☐
Was the venue clean, tidy and well maintained?	☐	☐	☐	☐
Were the staff helpful and friendly?	☐	☐	☐	☐
How comfortable were the meeting rooms?	☐	☐	☐	☐
If applicable, how would you rate the audio equipment?	☐	☐	☐	☐
If applicable, how would you rate the visual equipment?	☐	☐	☐	☐
How do you rate the training facilities and standards of the meeting rooms?	☐	☐	☐	☐
How do you rate the quality of the food and beverage?	☐	☐	☐	☐

Comments: ....

Client Name: (Optional) .... Name of Conference: ....
Date of Conference: .... Room Number: ....

Please leave this Questionnaire at Reception when you depart. Thank you.

Figure 2.20 A customer feedback form

from Aston Business School. This is for conference organisers and participants (as occasionally the views of organisers may vary from those of participants) to give immediate feedback on the facilities provided at the business school. Again, the form had postage prepaid.

While customers are vital sources of information for an organisation, many will also survey their own staff and management. This could be by means of a company image checklist or service level agreement. It could relate to a specific area, such as reception, or it might look at the organisation from a wider angle as in the example in Figure 2.21.

This type of survey may also set standards or 'benchmarks' to be followed. It is a valuable tool that can be used by internal or external customers to monitor and measure the quality of customer service. Each area would have criteria to meet, such as answering the telephone within three rings, greeting or acknowledging customers immediately on arrival at reception, etc.

AREAS OF OPERATIONS CONSIDERED IN A SERVICE LEVEL AGREEMENT COULD BE:	
Telephone answering	Speed Quality Switchboard/extension standards Number of times callers are re-routed Quality of message taking Telephonist's organisational knowledge
Reception	Greeting Speed of response Maintenance of area (comfort, interest, tidiness) Knowledge of organisation personnel/roles Quality of surroundings (noise/distractions)
Paperwork	Quality of general correspondence Quality and accuracy of literature
Written/verbal communication	Response times Understandability Accuracy of details Face-to-face – friendly, helpful, professional Company/product knowledge
Customer contacts	Quality of relationships built Frequency of contact with customers
Company structure/identity	Visibility to customer Clarity of organisation Who's who Consistency between departments/individuals Consistent company image
Location/access	Clear maps/directions Suggested route clear and easy to follow Clear, accurate signage No exposure to health and safety hazards

Figure 2.21 Service level agreement for the whole organisation

Suggestion box or comments book

These, again, may be used by internal or external customers, and may identify areas not previously considered by management. Some organisations used to have a 'complaints book', but this was seen as a negative approach, as well as a missed opportunity to receive developmental feedback or compliments. The trend now is for a 'comments book' that can be used to write in both positive and negative feedback. This is seen as less threatening by some customers than a survey, and more a case of volunteering information than being pressured to answer set questions.

Instead of writing in a book, customers can sometimes fill in a form like the one from Virgin Trains shown in Figure 2.22.

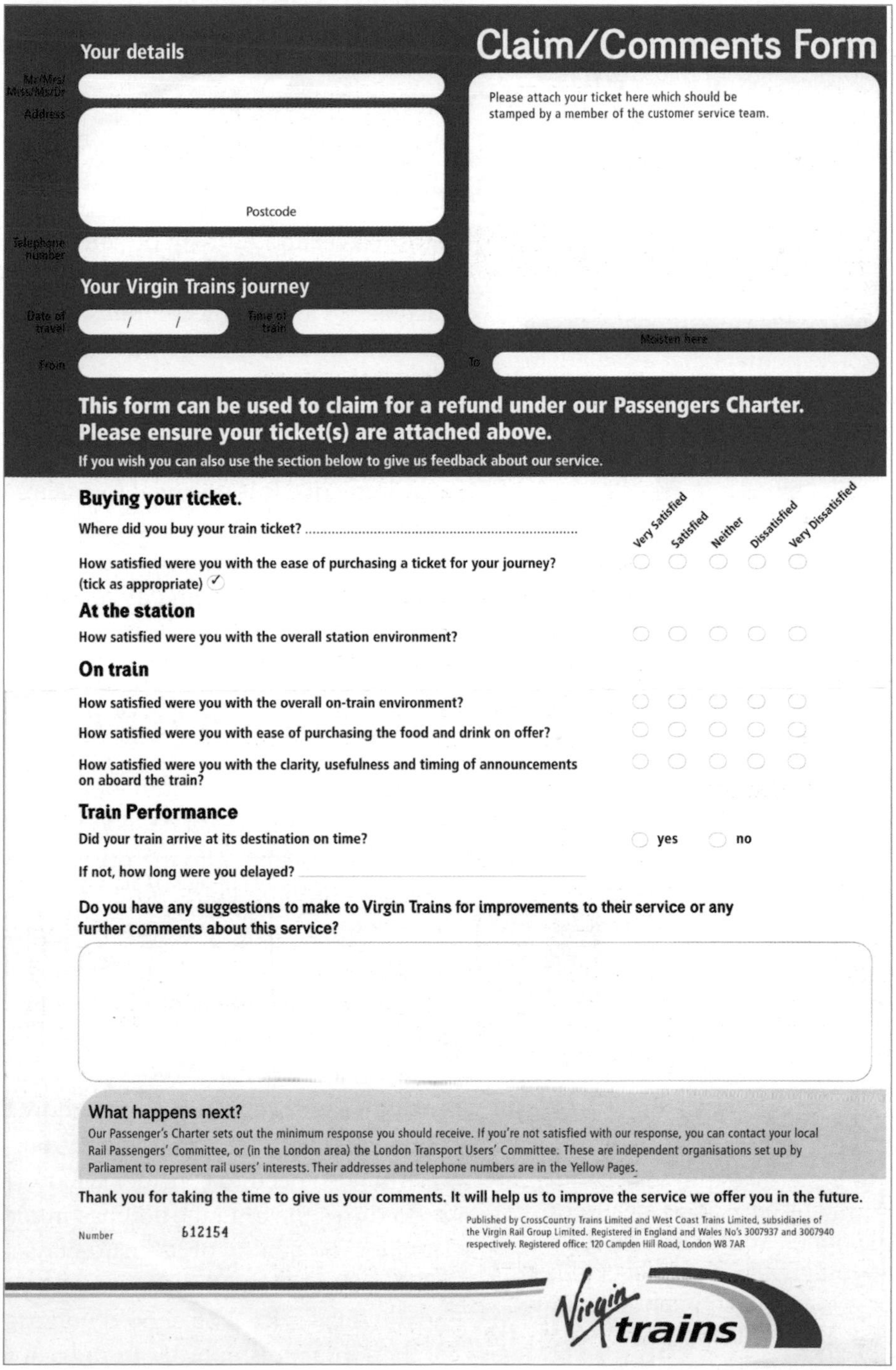

Claim/Comments Form

Your details

Mr/Mrs/Miss/Ms/Dr

Address

Postcode

Telephone number

Please attach your ticket here which should be stamped by a member of the customer service team.

Moisten here

Your Virgin Trains journey

Date of travel / /

Time of train

From

To

This form can be used to claim for a refund under our Passengers Charter.
Please ensure your ticket(s) are attached above.

If you wish you can also use the section below to give us feedback about our service.

Buying your ticket.

Where did you buy your train ticket? ....

	Very Satisfied	Satisfied	Neither	Dissatisfied	Very Dissatisfied
How satisfied were you with the ease of purchasing a ticket for your journey? (tick as appropriate) ✓	○	○	○	○	○
At the station					
How satisfied were you with the overall station environment?	○	○	○	○	○
On train					
How satisfied were you with the overall on-train environment?	○	○	○	○	○
How satisfied were you with ease of purchasing the food and drink on offer?	○	○	○	○	○
How satisfied were you with the clarity, usefulness and timing of announcements on aboard the train?	○	○	○	○	○

Train Performance

Did your train arrive at its destination on time? ○ yes ○ no

If not, how long were you delayed? ____________

Do you have any suggestions to make to Virgin Trains for improvements to their service or any further comments about this service?

What happens next?

Our Passenger's Charter sets out the minimum response you should receive. If you're not satisfied with our response, you can contact your local Rail Passengers' Committee, or (in the London area) the London Transport Users' Committee. These are independent organisations set up by Parliament to represent rail users' interests. Their addresses and telephone numbers are in the Yellow Pages.

Thank you for taking the time to give us your comments. It will help us to improve the service we offer you in the future.

Number 612154

Published by CrossCountry Trains Limited and West Coast Trains Limited, subsidiaries of the Virgin Rail Group Limited. Registered in England and Wales No's 3007937 and 3007940 respectively. Registered office: 120 Campden Hill Road, London W8 7AR

Virgin trains

Figure 2.22 A customer claim/comments form

Focus groups

An unusual type of focus group is used by Blackpool Pleasure Beach. The organisation has what is called a Junior Board, and to be a member of this one can apply through the Pleasure Beach's website. There are age restrictions, but members visit the park at least three times a year and carry out a review of rides and services. The points they raise are then discussed at a full board meeting with management of the Pleasure Beach, who take the views seriously. The point is that these are the customers now and in the future, and the Pleasure Beach must meet their expectations if it is to thrive. By focusing on youngsters at a theme park aimed at young people, any ideas are seen as relevant and will be considered by the management when new developments are planned.

Mystery shoppers

These may be independent people hired by the organisation to undertake a 'shopping exercise'. In other words they act as potential customers and then report back to the organisation on their findings. Occasionally, the mystery shopper will be an employee from another part of the organisation, not known to the employees in the facility being surveyed. He or she is asked to report back, usually on a pro forma, but occasionally in more detailed format, identifying any areas where service is weak or service is good and where improvements or developments can be made.

Assessment guidance

When you come to undertake the research for your assignment it might be a good idea to do this as a mystery shopper. You must take the role seriously as if you were a customer, and not a student preparing for an assignment. You are more likely to get a genuine response from the company on which to base your analysis.

Observation

Another form of feedback comes from observing the activities of the personnel in the organisation performing their usual duties and making notes of any specific areas that need to be considered. This may be undertaken by an internal colleague or a member of management, or it could be someone from another branch or department. All aspects of customer service should be covered, including body language, facial expressions, the quality and accuracy of information presented, and the attitude of the employee – as well as his or her performance of routine functions.

Conclusion

Most travel and tourism organisations undertake some form of customer care analysis, and may in fact use a variety of techniques in order to obtain an accurate reflection of what is happening in the organisation. The reports or findings need to be studied to identify areas for development, either in the procedures and practices or staff training requirements. It is essential to ensure that staff are maintaining the values and attitudes of the organisation as expressed in the mission statement, and are acting as good representatives of the organisation.

Preparation for assessment

In order to meet the requirements of Assessment Objectives 3 and 4 you have to undertake thorough research into the procedures and practices used by your chosen organisation to assess the effectiveness of its customer service before you can proceed to develop your analysis and evaluation. You should consider all the aspects of customer service as outlined in this unit in order to demonstrate that you understand the customer service principles and how they are applied by your chosen organisation.

You also need to consider what practices and procedures the organisation has in place to monitor the quality of its customer service provision and how these are used to develop the quality of service. You should undertake a review of these practices in order to suggest areas for development or improvement.

The following study and questions will set you on the right route to meeting the Assessment Objectives for this unit.

A study of Manchester Airport

Manchester Airport Group plc is the company that manages the airport. It is responsible for the buildings, taxiways, runways and land including car parks. It also makes sure the airport is safe to use by providing fire and security services. Other organisations, such as airlines and handling agents (referred to as service partners), are responsible for the many activities in and around the airport.

Customer service is the way in which Manchester Airport Group plc treats its customers, giving them what they want and need and making their experience enjoyable.

The customers of the airport are often assumed to be the passengers. But the only direct customers of the airport are the airlines, with their passengers being the end-users. There are other stakeholders in the customer chain – tour operators, the travel trade, service partners, employees and the general public. Service partners provide services such as catering, baggage handling, retail outlets, check-in facilities etc. They are also the internal customers of Manchester Airport. Service partner agreements are prepared as to service and quality required and signed by the airport management and the service partner.

Quality of service is checked regularly with meetings with service partners (who have their own customer service staff and policies), through surveys, analysing letters and telephone calls, face-to-face with employees on site, and comment cards from service partners. Checklists are used to monitor airport cleaning, which is contracted out. This is a computerised system and is the main tool used to assess the day-to-day cleaning operations. Specific standards are set for each of the 420 cleaning zones and there are three possible outcomes:

* not at the acceptable standard at the time of inspection

* meets the acceptable standard at the time of inspection

* exceeds the acceptable standard at the time of inspection.

Catering outlets and concessionaries have service agreements and contracts with Manchester Airport and these are monitored by the airport management. Contracts are agreed and signed and these include minimum delivery standards such as:

* retail units being kept in good repair

* Manchester Airport having 24-hour access for security and fire reasons

* all staff wearing an ID pass

* all concessionaries accepting credit cards.

Last year, Customer Relations received over 4500 comments and of these around 1000 were compliments or suggestions. The top two compliments received about the airport from passengers concerned the friendly and helpful staff and the wheelchair service. Complaints in the main related to catering, signage, baggage, terminal facilities, flight delays, car parking, the retail outlets, lack of waste bins and seating in the departure lounges.

An example of quality criteria as applied to Aviation Security officers is given below. The officers are assessed on the following criteria:

Makes no effort to discover who Security's customers are	1 2 3 4 5 6	Is aware of who Security's customers are
Does not exchange pleasantries	1 2 3 4 5 6	Gives a friendly, cheerful service
Displays a negative attitude to customers (e.g. surly, abrupt, unhelpful)	1 2 3 4 5 6	Consistently displays polite and helpful consideration in dealing with customers

Rating key:
1 unsuitable
2 falls short of requirements – considerable development needed
3 partially meets requirements – some development needed
4 meets requirements
5 does a little more than expected
6 exceeds requirements

Some of the criteria also given in the customer service policy include the following.

* Complaints by letter or telephone call have to be acknowledged within 3 working days.

* Complaints by letter or telephone call have to be dealt with effectively within 10 working days.

* Complaints by comment card are logged on to a database and replied to within 7 days.

* Telephone calls are directed to the appropriate department, company or service partner.

* Baggage is unloaded from aircraft within 15 minutes maximum (IATA standard).

* Maximum queuing time for Britannia and Monarch Airways is 15 minutes.

Theory into practice

1 Identify the customers of Manchester Airport Group plc, and state which are direct, and which are part of the customer service chain (stakeholders). Also classify them as either internal or external customers.

2 List the types of organisation classed as 'service providers'. What methods do Manchester Airport Group use to check the quality of service provided by these service providers?

3 What procedures are in place to monitor the performance of (a) cleaning contractors, (b) security personnel, and (c) dealing with complaints?

4 Explain why the airport sets minimum delivery standards with catering outlets and concessionaries.

5 Design an assessment tool that could be used to monitor the performance of a retail outlet, such as WH Smith, at the airport. Consider aspects such as opening times, staff presentation, cleanliness, availability and range of stock, speed of customer processing, queue management, layout of the outlet for access for all customer types, and any other criteria you feel are relevant.

Knowledge check

1 Explain the purpose of a mission statement.

2 Give *three* methods that organisations can use to measure the quality of customer service and explain the advantages and disadvantages of each.

3 Outline the benefits of staff training to the organisation in terms of efficiency and quality of customer service.

4 What is the difference between an external customer and an internal customer?

5 Identify at least *five* benefits to an organisation of providing excellent customer service.

6 Explain the customer needs of a group of Italian tourists visiting a museum.

7 Handling complaints requires practice and skill. What skills would you be expected to use when handling a complaint or dealing with a problem?

8 Explain the term 'value for money' when used in relation to customer service situations.

9 How can an organisation try to maintain consistency and reliability in the provision of its customer service?

10 Tone and vocabulary are important in customer service situations. Explain this in relation to dealing with customers face-to-face.

Resources

You can collect information and opinions about customer service from many sources. Here are some suggestions:

* regional tourist boards for Welcome Host training

* 'fly on the wall' TV documentaries such as 'Airport'

* television comedy programmes such as 'Fawlty Towers' and 'Brittas Empire'

* case studies in books such as this one

* websites of major travel and tourism organisations, such as Marriott Hotels, Thomson, Alton Towers, the National Trust, and so on (use a search engine such as Google to locate websites).

UNIT 3

Travel destinations

Introduction

Government statistics show that the British are travelling abroad more than ever before. Although the proportion of UK residents who did not take a holiday of four days or more has remained relatively unchanged over the past three decades, the proportion taking two or more holidays has increased from 15 to 25 per cent.

Between 1982 and 2002, the number of visits abroad made by residents of the UK almost tripled. However, spending on these visits in 2002 was more than seven times the spending in 1982. In real terms (taking inflation into account) UK residents' spending quadrupled over the 20 years. In 2003, visits overseas by UK residents rose by over 3 per cent to an all-time high of 61.5 million.

People travel for many reasons and it is usual to find both domestic and overseas visits being made for one of the following:

* leisure travel, such as a family holiday or short break
* business travel, such as attending a meeting, conference or an event
* to visit close family, relatives and friends.

The most common reason is for leisure purposes and for many people the summer holiday has become a well established highlight of the year. The actual selection of a holiday destination has become, for many of us, a major activity in itself.

How you will be assessed

This unit is assessed through your portfolio work. You will investigate *two* travel destinations, one of which is short-haul and one long-haul. You must show that you are familiar with the use of destination maps at different scales and are aware of how these can be used to display locational information. You must show an understanding of how the features of particular destinations appeal to different types of visitor. You will also have to show evidence that you have used various sources of information and how these provide clues about future tourism development.

What you need to learn

* the geographical location of major short-haul and long-haul destinations that attract UK tourists
* the key features of the major destinations
* the reasons why these features make destinations appeal to different tourist groups
* the reasons why some destinations may become more popular in the future whilst others will decline in popularity.

The choice of destination

Before we look at travel destinations themselves, it is important to recognise some of the influences that are at work when an individual traveller makes a decision to visit any particular location.

There are many forces at work that can influence our decision whether or not we will even consider visiting a particular destination. Several of these forces are depicted in Figure 3.1. However, our perceptions about places are often influenced mostly by the way in which we first hear about them. Furthermore, our perceptions can frequently be wrong, and we can easily form impressions about destinations that do not reflect a true image of the reality.

For most people the preferred way of spending their leisure time is to take a complete break from everyday life and to go on holiday, either within the United Kingdom or abroad.

Popular destinations

According to the World Tourism Organisation, by the year 2020 China will become the world's favourite destination – it is estimated that a total of 137 million people will visit the country. Germans are expected to be the world's most travelled people at that time with 163 million visits, or 10 per cent of the world market. The Chinese will be fourth, closely followed by the British who will make a total of 96 million trips. Figure 3.2 shows popular overseas destinations for UK travellers.

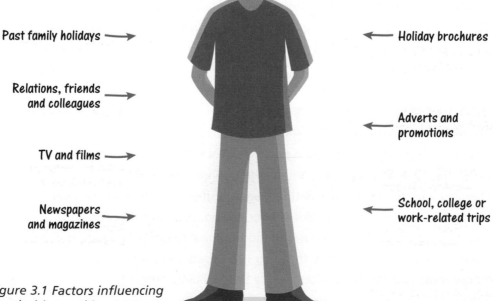

Past family holidays ⟶

Relations, friends and colleagues ⟶

TV and films ⟶

Newspapers and magazines ⟶

⟵ Holiday brochures

⟵ Adverts and promotions

⟵ School, college or work-related trips

Figure 3.1 Factors influencing the decision-making process

SHORT HAUL		LONG HAUL			
Spain	Netherlands	Thailand	UAE	Barbados	China
France	Cyprus	Maldives	Mauritius	St Lucia	India
Greece	Belgium	USA	Singapore	Mexico	Jamaica
Italy	Germany	Sri Lanka	Malaysia	Antigua	South Africa
Portugal	Malta	Egypt	Kenya	Australia	New Zealand
Irish Republic	Austria	Hong Kong	Indonesia	Cuba	
Turkey					

Figure 3.2 Popular overseas destinations for UK travellers

Theory into practice

On a blank outline map of the world, name and locate each country listed in Figure 3.2. Then set up and complete the following table:

COUNTRY	CAPITAL	AIRPORT	CURRENCY	RESORT OR DESTINATION	RISK OR HAZARD
UAE	Abu Dhabi	Abu Dhabi	Dirham	Dubai	Heatstroke
		Dubai			
Spain	Madrid	Madrid	Euro	Salou	Seawater pollution
		Barcelona			
Australia	Canberra	Sydney	Dollar	Cairns	Bush fires

Influences on the choice of destination

All of us make decisions about where and when we are going to travel. Our final choice of destination to visit and details of our final travel arrangements are subject to a complex set of inter-relationships. Each individual traveller has certain constraints that, in effect, limit his or her ability to choose from the full range of alternatives that are currently available to the UK travelling public. Individual preferences will be subject to factors such as those illustrated in Figure 3.3.

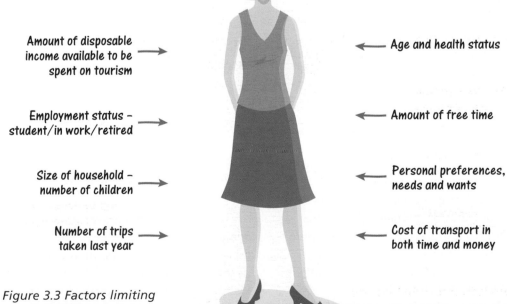

Amount of disposable income available to be spent on tourism →

Employment status – student/in work/retired →

Size of household – number of children →

Number of trips taken last year →

← Age and health status

← Amount of free time

← Personal preferences, needs and wants

← Cost of transport in both time and money

Figure 3.3 Factors limiting our destination choice

Use Figures 3.1 and 3.3 to help you suggest reasons why people with similar interests and preferences will visit very different destinations (as shown in Figure 3.4) in order to satisfy their requirements.

SEASIDE	NATIONAL PARK RECREATION	MOUNTAIN ADVENTURE	CITY BREAK
Southend-on-sea	Yorkshire Dales	Lake District	Chester
Benidorm	Ireland	The Alps	Amsterdam
Lanzarote	Canada	Norway	Rome
Barbados	Costa Rica	The Andes	New York
Fiji	New Zealand	The Himalayas	Sydney

Figure 3.4 Destinations for particular types of leisure holiday

People react in different ways to the opportunities available, even if their personal circumstances are virtually identical. Most people would like the 'perfect holiday', one that is tailor-made to satisfy every wish and desire. In reality we know that such a situation is most unlikely to arise, so we are content with a holiday that meets most of our personal requirements. In other words, most people are quite happy to behave as satisficers rather than optimisers. The operation of such influencing factors helps to explain the destination choices made by the UK travelling public.

Tourist destinations actively try to increase the number of visitors. Tourism is one of the world's biggest industries, with international tourism receipts now approaching the equivalent of 400 billion US dollars worldwide. Furthermore, these receipts have grown by 12 per cent a year over the last decade, and competition between countries for tourists' spending looks set to become even more intense. All destinations will therefore be trying to develop a consistent and high-quality tourism product to maximise their appeal and thus maintain the very valuable economic impacts that tourism can bring.

Leading tourism locations receive considerable benefits from their visitor numbers, so it is no surprise that established destinations like New York, Hong Kong and Dubai experience a significant contribution to their gross domestic product (GDP) from this sector. In an attempt to manage and sustain tourism growth, many countries have established specific development plans for the tourism sector.

In the UK, 'destination benchmarking' surveys are undertaken to update information from previous surveys on the profile behaviour and opinions of tourists in order to identify emerging trends. These surveys include the regional tourist boards' standard 'destination benchmarking' questions which are designed to measure levels of satisfaction with particular destinations. This allows comparisons to be made with competing destinations in terms of key variables such as:

* accommodation
* parking
* attractions
* places to eat and drink
* shops
* ease of finding one's way around
* public toilets
* cleanliness of streets
* upkeep of parks and open spaces
* choice of nightlife/entertainment
* overall impression
* security from crime
* safety from traffic
* overall enjoyment
* likelihood of recommending it to others.

All tourist destinations, whether in the UK or overseas, recognise that each potential visitor has available a choice of options. Each location is therefore in direct competition with many similar destinations. Variations in the quality of total visitor experience will result in variations in visitor numbers. The competing destinations will battle for our custom on three key fronts:

* quality – its beauty/uniqueness, levels of service and infrastructure

* price – of accommodation, transport and catering

* level of promotion – the ways in which the destination can be brought to the attention of potential visitors.

The geographical location of destinations

Any study of the world's travel and tourism industry will at some stage involve knowledge about where places are to be found. It is important that people who work in travel and tourism have a clear idea about the world's basic geography.

The position of any location on the Earth's surface can be described in terms of its *latitude*, measured in degrees, north or south of the Equator. This is very similar to the lines of *longitude*, which indicate the position east or west of Greenwich in London. The furthest point north is the North Pole (90°N) and the furthest point south is the South Pole (90°S). In each hemisphere, there are two additional important lines of latitude between the Pole and the Equator – these are the Tropic of Cancer (23.5°N) and the Tropic of Capricorn (23.5°S). The Arctic Circle is at 66.5°N and the Antarctic Circle is at 66.5°S.

The *lines of latitude* indicate divisions that allow us to make generalisations about the locational position of all points on the Earth's surface. It is quite common to see reference being made to the following:

* equatorial latitudes – between 5 degrees north and south of the Equator

* tropical latitudes – anywhere between 23.5 degrees north and south of the Equator

* sub-tropical latitudes – between 23.5 and approximately 30 degrees north and south of the Equator

* temperate latitudes – between approximately 30 and 50 degrees north and south of the Equator

* arctic latitudes – around 66.5 degrees north and south of the Equator

* polar latitudes – anywhere between the Poles and 66.5 degrees north and south.

Using and developing your research skills

All people working in the travel and tourism industry need to be able to find out about places because they will have to answer questions from prospective customers. This information has to be *up to date* and *accurate*. There is a wide range of sources of information. Being able to answer questions and supply accurate information is part of delivering good customer service.

When students or researchers want to get information on a topic, there is an orderly manner in which the investigation should be approached.

For the assessment of this unit you will be expected to show that you have:

- been clear what you are trying to find out
- been able to understand how to search for information
- been clear in deciding what might be useful
- presented the information obtained in an orderly way that is fit for its purpose
- drawn conclusions from the information that you have obtained
- acknowledged your sources of information, thus allowing for further references to be made.

You are also expected to choose appropriate sources of information.

A wide range of organisations provide information for anyone who wants to travel to virtually any destination in the world. Travel organisations can be categorized in terms of whether they are primarily marketing or non-marketing. Marketing organisations include tour operators, tourist boards and the overseas marketing departments of the destinations themselves. While any information about a destination can be of use to a particular individual, it is always worth remembering that the primary objective of marketing and promotion departments is to attract tourists who are able to spend money on their product or at their destination.

The amount of information that is currently available about most destinations for most travellers usually far exceeds what is required, so the problem is where to start.

Brochures

Most people planning a leisure trip will visit a local travel agency. Here they can find a wide range of brochures that are often arranged according to the type of holiday. There may be a section on cruises, sections arranged by country, types of package such as villas and self-catering breaks, special interest holidays such as skiing, coach tours and a host of others. There will also be brochures produced by transport providers such as ferry companies or airlines giving details

not only of their transport services but also of their particular range of inclusive tours. British travel agents distribute between six and ten brochures per person booking a holiday.

Brochures are a very good source of basic information about particular destinations. It is common to find the following included:

- ✱ a map giving the location of the destination relative to point of entry, together with resort attractions
- ✱ a table of climate figures indicating what the weather conditions will be like
- ✱ photographs showing aspects of the natural and built environment that people are likely to be interested in
- ✱ a description of the facilities to be found in selected types of destination accommodation
- ✱ brief details of local places of interest and attractions.

Guides and manuals

It must be remembered that the main purpose of glossy printed brochures is to create *awareness* amongst readers which will then lead to a positive decision to buy one of the featured holiday products. This will not be sufficient for anyone wanting to make a detailed study of the attractions to be found within a particular destination.

Travellers wanting to know more about particular destinations have a number of options. Travel agency staff should have immediate access to a selection of guides and manuals such as the OAG *Flight Guide*, OAG *Cruise and Ferry Guide*, OAG *Gazetteers*, OAG *Holiday Guides* and the OAG *Guide to International Travel*. They will be able to refer to these to answer specific questions about particular destinations. Travel employees cannot be expected to know the answer to every question but they should know where to look in order to obtain appropriate information. For example, the OAG *Gazetteers* contain independent reviews of resorts and accommodation in six volumes covering the following:

- ✱ Mediterranean hotels
- ✱ Mediterranean apartments

* European cities

* long-haul

* North America

* ski, lakes and mountains.

Both private individuals and agency staff can use the Columbus Press *World Travel Guide*. This is a huge publication and includes everything that travel staff will need to answer a general destination enquiry from a member of the public. The contents range from details of the climate in locations at a specific time to the social and cultural background of the destination. Information is provided about many destinations on a country-by-country basis, and an extract is shown in Figure 3.5. Further reference will be made to the Caribbean island of Dominica in a case study later in this chapter.

National Tourist Boards

Anyone who intends visiting a country can write to the relevant tourist board and ask for information. Most countries publish marketing brochures and leaflets that provide more detailed information than the tour operator's brochure,

usually including details about climate, social conditions and currency regulations. Furthermore, because the UK is such an important generator of outbound tourists, many national tourist boards maintain a UK office to service this potential demand. The range of material available is sometimes quite impressive and we can look at an actual example to illustrate this point further.

The Government of Dubai operates a Department of Tourism & Commerce Marketing (DTCM). The DTCM actively promotes Dubai's tourism product and brings it to the attention of a global marketplace in an attempt to sustain and extend the number of visitors that the destination currently attracts. The DTCM has established a global network of overseas offices to aid its promotional strategy and in 2004 the following locations were operational:

DTCM in Dubai (www.dubaitourism.ae)
New York – North America
London – UK and Ireland
Paris – France
Frankfurt/Main – Germany
Stockholm – Scandinavia

Dominica (Commonwealth of)

ACCOMMODATION

HOTELS: The number of hotels has expanded in recent years; most of the hotels are small- to medium-sized, and well-equipped; the largest of them has 98 rooms. There are three hotels at the fringe of an area designated as a National Park. Information can be obtained from the Dominica Hotel Association, PO Box 384, Roseau. Tel: 448 6565. Fax: 448 0299. The Association also provides assistance in organising conferences and conventions in Dominica. **Grading:** Many of the hotels offer accommodation according to one of a number of 'Plans' widely used in the Caribbean; these include Modified American Plan (MAP) which consists of room, breakfast and dinner and European Plan (EP) which consists of room only.
APARTMENTS/COTTAGES: These offer self-catering, full service and maid service facilities and are scattered around the island.
GUEST-HOUSES: There is a variety of guest-houses and inns around the island which offer a comfortable and very friendly atmosphere. There is a 10% government tax and 10% service charge on rooms.
CAMPING/CARAVANNING: Not encouraged at the present time, though sites may be designated in future. Overnight safari tours are run by local operators.

RESORTS & EXCURSIONS

Roseau, on the southwest coast, is the main centre for visitors. From hotels around here it is possible to arrange jeep safari tours for seeing the hinterland of the country. Canoe trips up the rivers can also be arranged. The beaches are mainly of black volcanic sand, but there are a few white-sand beaches on the northeast of this island. Sports facilities include scuba diving, sailing and sport fishing.
Morne Trois Pitons National Park, covering 7000 hectares (17,000 acres) in the south-central part of Dominica, was established in July 1975. Places of interest in the park include the *Boiling Lake,* the second-largest in the world which was discovered in 1922, and the *Emerald Pool, Middleham Falls, Sari Sari Falls, Trafalgar Triple Waterfalls, Freshwater Lake, Boeri Lake* and the *Valley of Desolation.*
Cabrits Historical Park was designated a park in 1987. Attractions include the **Cabrits Peninsular** which contains the historical ruins of *Fort Shirley* and *Fort George,* 18th- and early 19th-century forts, and a museum at Fort Shirley. The usual touring spots in addition to the above include the **Carib Indian Territory,** the *Sulphur Springs,* the *Central Forest Reserve, Botanical Gardens, Titou Gorge, L'Escalier Tête Chien,* several areas of rainforest and a variety of fauna and flora.

Figure 3.5 Information on the island of Dominica, which is looked at again later in this chapter, taken from the World Travel Guide *published by Columbus Travel Guides.*

Milan – Italy
Zurich – Switzerland and Austria
Moscow – Russian Federation, CIS and Baltic states
Johannesburg – South Africa
Mumbai – India
Hong Kong – China and Far East
Tokyo – Japan
Sydney – Australia and New Zealand

The DTCM produces a wide variety of promotional materials, including maps, destination guides and brochures that will attract leisure and business visitors. It produces information for a series of niche markets using titles such as:

The Classic Golf Destination
The Watersports Resort
Tours and Safaris
The Birdwatcher's Paradise
The Great Incentive
Heritage and Culture
Dubai: Cruise Hub of the Arabian Gulf
Conference and Exhibition Facilities

The worldwide promotional activities of the DTCM are widely credited with being one of the key elements in Dubai's current tourism boom. The government agency has won international awards and recognition as the leading exponent of destination marketing in the Middle East and it has become a model to be emulated by other destinations. We shall return to Dubai later in a case study.

Travel guides

Travel guides give a comprehensive coverage of destinations all over the world. Country and regional guides, such as those produced by Rough Guides and distributed worldwide by the Penguin group, include recommendations from shoestring to luxury and cover more than 200 destinations around the globe, including almost every country in the Americas and Europe, more than half of Africa and most of Asia and Australasia. Rough Guides also produce city guides which provide neighbourhood information and contain easy-to-use coloured maps for streets and city transport.

Lonely Planet is a similar source and it publishes over 650 guidebooks, in fourteen different languages, covering every corner of the planet. The organisation also offers a range of services to aid and inspire travellers at home or on the road. Many travel publishers publish pocket-sized city and country guides that are more suitable for short stays or business trips. Most travel guides have excellent photographs illustrating the culture and attractions of the destination.

Trade journals, newspapers and magazines

Trade journals such as *Travel Trade Gazette* and *Travel Weekly* contain a lot of information about destinations. Here the focus is on new developments and what is being planned or introduced into various tour operators' programmes, with comments about how sales to the travelling public might be affected. There are up-to-the-minute commentaries on featured destinations, and details of road shows and the various incentives available for travel agency front-line staff.

Newspapers and magazines frequently contain destination reports within their travel sections. These will feature best-value options and other advice for readers contemplating either a domestic or an overseas trip. Figure 3.6 shows an illustration about Barcelona, a destination that is the subject of a case study later. The significant point about this particular extract is that it clearly aims its advice at a range of visitor types. In terms of Barcelona being a visitor destination, the extract emphasises that travellers with a variety of needs and wants can be catered for by a range of local providers.

Television

Television programmes have featured reports about holiday destinations for over 40 years. Several programmes, such as the BBC's 'Holiday Programme' and ITV's 'Wish You Were Here', have introduced more than one generation of leisure travellers to the delights of locations scattered throughout the tourist world. Furthermore, the locational setting of particular programmes and films has increased viewer awareness as to the attractions contained in many destinations. Indeed, the visiting of locations featured on both the big and small screens has fuelled tourism development at various destinations.

In addition, over three million people make use of teletext as a source of information on their holiday arrangements.

BARCELONA

Where to stay, where to eat, what to do: Barcelona for every budget

ON THE CHEAP

Enter Hostal Oliva (Passeig de Gracia 32; 00 34-93 488 0162) through a traditional Modernista atrium. Rooms 10 and 11 are nice ensuite doubles (if you're okay with the traffic hum) — good value at £41, room-only. Hostal Fontanella (Via Laietana 71; 93 317 5943) is all flowery fabrics, gilt-edged mirrors and frilly armrests: a homely atmosphere, but you'll need to bone up on your Spanish. Ensuite doubles cost £48.

Can Culleretes (Carrer Quintana 5; 93 317 3022; closed Sunday evening and July) is Barcelona's oldest restaurant, serving meaty treats such as suckling pig in apricots and prunes (£8) and wild boar and game stew (£5). Or try Les Quinze Nits (93 317 3075), on the north side of the beautiful Placa Reial. It offers Catalan cuisine at Happy Meal prices (sausage with white beans costs just £3), but you have to queue for ages if you time it wrongly.

Get some salt in your hair with a sun-beaten stroll along the beach promenade. Bathe if you dare, but there are cleaner beaches up the coast. This one is better for eating and drinking beside.

MIDDLE OF THE ROAD

Nestled between two leafy, cafe-filled squares in the Barri Gotic is Hotel Jardi (Placa Sant Josep Oriol 1; 00 34-93 301 5900; doubles from £58). Rooms are basic — a little poky, but spotless — and the location is ideal. The brand-new and supertrendy Hotel Constanza (Bruc 33; 93 270 1910, www.hotelconstanza.com) is excellent value at £83 a double. Seven new rooms with sun terraces should be ready this autumn.

Agua (Passeig Maritim 30; 93 225 1272) is a bargain by the beach. Try seafood specialities such as sweet shrimps with tagliolini, garlic and chilli (£5). Or be entirely unmodern: reserve a downstairs window table at the Catalan classic El Gran Cafe (Avinyo 9; 93 318 7986) and order the duck with pear (£11).

The Palau de la Musica Catalana (Sant Francesc de Paula 2; 93 295 7200, www.palaumusica.org; closed Monday; £6) has an opulent stained-glass ceiling and an intricately decorated interior. Seeing it without music is pointless, so go to a concert if you have time. Tickets start at about £20.

NO EXPENSE SPARED

The Prestige Hotel (Paseo de Gracia 62; 00 34-93 272 4180; executive doubles from £190) lives up to its name. Near the Gaudi facades of La Pedrera and Casa Batllo, it does modern decor in a classic building. And the minibar's free. The central location of the supertasteful Hotel Neri (93 304 0655; www.hotelneri.com) doesn't mean it's noisy, and the doubles are a steal at £127.

El Bulli (Cala Montjoi; 97 215 0457, www.elbulli.com) is, relatively speaking, just around the corner, on the Costa Brava — and, as one of the world's top restaurants, it should not be missed. But tables book up for a whole season in one day in January, so chances are that it will be. Chin up — there are many other wonderful options, including the seafood emporium Botafumeiro (Carrer Gran de Gracia 81; 93 218 4230), where the extravagant shellfish platter for two costs £70.

A night at the opera. Gran Teatre del Liceu (93 485 9913, www.liceubarcelona.com) has been fully restored after the fire of 1994. The best tickets start at about £40.

Souce: Harriet Perry from *The Sunday Times*, 5 September 2004

Figure 3.6 Information on Barcelona, which is looked at again later in this chapter

The Internet

Internet research of holiday destinations is now commonplace. Over 25 million people currently investigate aspects of their domestic and overseas travel in this way. Many people have access at work, home or via a third party, and most travel and tourism organisations maintain a website for information storage and to service the increasing trend for on-line bookings.

The amount of data available is extremely large and information about most destinations in the world can be found at the click of a mouse. However, some sites are more useful than others, so 'surfing the net' can easily become a very time-consuming and tiring process. It is for this reason that face-to-face contact with a travel advisor remains popular with members of the travelling public.

Five destinations around the world

Assessment guidance

Assessment Objectives 2, 3 and 4 for this unit require you to have made a study of *two* contrasting destinations. You have to examine the key features of each destination and explain how and why they appeal to different visitor types. You will use a range of sources to obtain information about each and then analyse your findings, leading to a reasoned explanation about future trends.

One way in which it is possible to examine the reasons behind the growth of certain locations as important travel and tourism destinations is to look at case studies. The rapid growth and expansion of Dubai as a tourist destination is a very good illustration.

Destination: Dubai

The United Arab Emirates (UAE) comprises seven members: Abu Dhabi (the capital city), Dubai, Sharjah, Ajman, Umm Al Quwain, Ras Al Khaimah and Fujairah. Dubai, with an area of 3885 square kilometres, is the second largest emirate. Dubai is situated on the banks of the Dubai Creek, a natural inlet from the Arabian Gulf, which divides the city into the Deira district to its north, and Bur Dubai to its south. The city ranks as the UAE's most important port and commercial centre. Along the Arabian Gulf coast there are offshore islands, coral reefs and sabkha (salt marshes). Stretches of gravel plain and sandy desert characterise the inland region. To the east, a range of mountains lies close to the Gulf of Oman and forms a backbone through the Mussandam Peninsula. The western interior of the country, most of it in Abu Dhabi, consists mainly of desert interspersed with oases.

The emirate embraces a wide variety of scenery in a very small area. In a single day, the tourist can experience everything from rugged mountains and awe-inspiring sand dunes to sandy beaches and lush green parks, from dusty villages to luxurious residential districts, and from ancient houses with wind towers to ultra-modern shopping malls. Having expanded along both banks of the Creek, Dubai's central business district is divided into two parts – Deira on the northern side and Bur Dubai to the south – connected by a tunnel and two bridges. Each has its share of fine mosques and busy souks, of public buildings, shopping malls, hotels, office towers, banks, hospitals, schools, apartments and villas.

Outside this core, the city extends to the neighbouring emirate of Sharjah to the north, while extending south and west in a long ribbon of development alongside the Gulf, through the districts of Satwa, Jumeirah and Umm Suqeim. At first glance, the city presents a predominantly modern face, an ever-changing skyline of new developments, from striking glass and concrete towers to gracious modern buildings incorporating traditional Arabian architectural motifs and features.

Statistics

Some of the statistics surrounding Dubai's recent developments are particularly impressive and few locations in the world can match the degree of economic diversification that the emirate has achieved in a short space of time (see Figure 3.7).

Figure 3.7 Key events in the development of Dubai as a tourist and business destination

DATE	DEVELOPMENT MILESTONE	
1971	The foundation of the United Arab Emirates 	
1979	World's largest artificial port opens at Jebel Ali	
1985	The Jebel Ali Free Zone opens Award-winning airline Emirates is established 	
1989	The Dubai Desert Classic, a European PGA tournament, tees off for the first time 	
1990	Five million passengers pass through Dubai International Airport 	
1993	Tourists exceed one million	
1996	First running of the Dubai World Cup, the world's richest horse race, at Nad Al Sheba First annual Dubai Shopping Festival attracts millions of visitors 	

Continued

DATE	DEVELOPMENT MILESTONE	
1998	Tourists exceed two million	
1999	World's only 7-star hotel, the Burj Al Arab, opens and the landmark Emirates Towers come into operation	
2000	Dubai Internet City established, attracting the world's top IT firms including IBM, Microsoft and HP Sheikh Rashid Terminal developed at Dubai International Airport completing the first phase of a US$ 450 million expansion Second phase due for completion in 2007 raising annual capacity to 60 million visitors	
2001	Dubai Media City opens, becoming the regional home of global media giants such as CNN and Reuters Construction begins of The Palm, the world's largest artificial islands Tourists exceed three million	
2002	Emirates announces plans to double its fleet of aircraft by 2007 Tourists exceed 4.5 million Dubai International Airport handles 16 million passengers	
2003	UAE first Middle Eastern country to host meetings of the World Bank and the IMF, in Dubai Dubai International Financial Centre opens Dubai Healthcare City opens Burj Dubai, the world's tallest tower, is announced Dubailand, the region's ultimate tourism, leisure and entertainment destination, is announced	 دبي لاند Dubailand

In 1989, Dubai recorded only 630 000 visitor arrivals but numbers increased to over 8 million in 2003, with at least 458 000 coming from the UK. Dubai has managed to increase its number of visitors by over 1200 per cent in little more than a decade and tourism is now, at 12 per cent of the gross domestic product (GDP), one of the emirate's more important and fastest growing sectors of the economy.

Dubai's significance as a global destination stems from the fact that it can be viewed from two main perspectives. It is not just a simple holiday destination, it is an important commercial, trading and business centre as well. Therefore visitors to Dubai provide examples of the three categories into which tourists are usually divided. A recent visitor survey in Dubai identified the following figures:

* leisure visitors – 44 per cent
* business visitors – 45 per cent
* visiting friends and relatives (VFR) – 8 per cent
* not classified – 3 per cent.

Previously viewed in tourism terms as little more than a 'duty-free stopover', Dubai today has become a highly acclaimed destination offering an outstanding range of facilities and services for both leisure and business travellers. We next look at some of the reasons behind Dubai's phenomenal growth.

Features

Figure 3.8 shows Dubai's geographical location (55°E, 25°N) on the southern shore of the Arabian Gulf. It is strategically located at the crossroads of three continents – Europe, Asia and Africa – a natural meeting place. Dubai is now a major aviation hub. The government's 'open skies' policy has resulted in Dubai International Airport being served by some 105 airlines, with connections to more than 140 cities worldwide. It is also the operational hub for the Emirates airline and so attracts visitors wanting a stopover. The UK is particularly well served with nearly 70 scheduled non-stop flights a week from Heathrow, Gatwick, Manchester, Birmingham and Glasgow. This high degree of accessibility, so important for the development of tourism, is clearly one factor in explaining the particularly high increase in UK visitors to Dubai between 1989 (only 32 000) and 2003 (over 400 000).

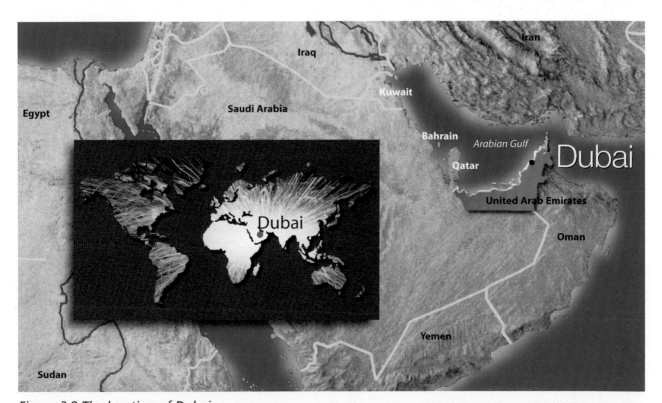

Figure 3.8 The location of Dubai

Dubai has a very accessible location. In terms of flying times, London is seven hours away, Frankfurt is six, Hong Kong eight and Nairobi four. These facts give Dubai a very wide catchment area. Business events in Dubai attract delegates and trade visitors from around the world. This catchment area covers the Gulf states, other Arab countries like Iran, the Asian subcontinent, East Africa, Central Asia and the CIS. This rapidly developing region boasts a population of around 1.5 billion people. A recent analysis of Dubai hotel guests identified the following breakdown:

* Europe – 27.3 per cent

* Asia – 22.4 per cent

* Gulf states – 20.2 per cent

* other Arab states – 10.4 per cent

* UAE – 6.8 per cent

* Africa – 6.3 per cent

* America – 4.6 per cent

* Australia and Pacific – 1.5 per cent

Dubai was also well placed to take advantage of the increasing global trend for leisure travel and to provide a different experience for an increasingly adventurous travelling public who constantly demand alternative destinations. The emirate contained a mix of natural and cultural attractions that formed the basis of a very marketable leisure tourism product. The existing natural attractions included:

* miles of clean uncrowded beaches along the shores of the Arabian Gulf

* a sub-tropical climate with average temperatures of 18°C in January, 33°C in July and annual precipitation of less than 150 mm, contributing to a year-long tourist season

* the availability of watersports all year round in the Gulf (and the Gulf of Oman is a diving centre of international significance)

* desert dunes for a variety of outdoor activities and leisure pursuits

* the Hatta Mountains for 'wadi-bashing' and other adventurous pursuits

* the Al Maha environmental conservation reserve, the base for the reintroduction of the Arabian Oryx.

Dubai is a migratory crossroads in both spring and autumn for many bird species. The Khor Dubai Wildlife Sanctuary is home to more than 1000 Greater Flamingos.

Dubai also had a strong cultural heritage to exploit for tourism purposes. Important elements of this cultural attractiveness to Western visitors included:

* the 'exotic' Middle Eastern atmosphere associated with the hustle and bustle of the souks and dhow wharves along Dubai Creek

* the distinctly Middle Eastern architecture of the wind towers, mosques and palaces

* the traditional welcoming and hospitable culture of the Arab world

* acceptance of a cosmopolitan lifestyle.

Although these natural and cultural assets have clearly contributed to Dubai's success as a destination, it is very important to emphasise that they have been greatly enhanced by ambitious investment in the tourism infrastructure on the part of both public and private sectors.

The Dubai government's Department of Tourism & Commerce Marketing (DTCM) is the main organisation for the promotion and development of tourism in the emirate. The department has taken over the licensing of hotels, hotel apartments, tour operators, tourist transport companies and travel agents. It has a supervisory role covering all tourist, archaeological and heritage sites, tourism conferences and exhibitions, the operation of tourism information services and the licensing and organisation of tour guides. The government provides ongoing development to the infrastructure, and the recent opening of the Port Rashid cruise line terminal is just one of a series of innovations aimed at widening the total tourism product base within Dubai. It is hoped that this terminal will do for cruising what the opening of Dubai Duty Free did for air traffic arrivals. The government has a direct stake in the tourism sector through the development and ownership of a number of the major hotels as well as spectacular theme parks such as 'Wild Wadi'. This investment is not just a matter of expenditure; it is clearly demonstrating that quality must be paramount.

Think it over ...

Identify the various ways in which destinations can demonstrate the quality of their various tourism facilities. For example, what quality standards are available in the UK?

The recent creation of the 7-star luxury Burj Al Arab Hotel is yet another illustration of this underpinning philosophy in the emirate's development. Government commitment to the tourism industry is further indicated by the fact that His Highness Sheikh Mohammed bin Rashid Al Maktoum, Crown Prince of Dubai and UAE Minister of Defence, is not only the DTCM Chairman but he has been the driving force behind many of the emirate's most spectacular development schemes. This level of government commitment to the tourism industry has helped to generate significant private sector investment. Hotel and apartment complexes have been extensively developed. There has been a rapid expansion in the number of local inbound tour operators offering a range of tourist experiences from 4-by-4 desert safaris to dhow cruises.

For example, the majesty and tranquillity of the desert can now be experienced in a choice of exciting half-day, full-day and overnight safaris. These action-packed trips cover varied terrain ranging from desert to mountain and frequently include remote camel and goat farms as well as isolated villages. Highlights of a Dubai desert safari will usually include the following:

✳ dune driving in four-wheel-drive vehicles (see Figure 3.9)

✳ wadi-bashing – exploring the wadis or dry beds of streams that flow after the winter rains from the Hajar mountains, with the option of a

Figure 3.9 Dune driving in Dubai

swim in one of the many rock pools (see Figure 3.10)

✳ sand-skiing, using special skis to negotiate the slopes of high dunes in the emirate's interior

✳ camel riding, a major tourist attraction.

Other attractions are desert feasts, which are popular with visitors as an evening activity. A traditional Arabian barbecue under the stars follows spectacular sunset views. These can be tailored to meet every taste from a romantic

Figure 3.10 Wadi-bashing in Dubai

peaceful experience to elaborate fun-packed evenings complete with music, belly-dancing and displays of falconry. Some operators offer the opportunity to experience the traditional desert way of life in a Bedouin village outside Dubai.

The result of these various developments has been the creation of a world-class tourism product for a world-class destination. We can now look in more detail at the nature of Dubai's built attractions in an attempt to identify the ingredients of a successful destination.

Built attractions

A recent survey of UK tour operators promoting Dubai identified sport as being a significant component of the destination's appeal. The findings of this survey indicated that:

* 65 per cent offered golfing holidays

* 10 per cent had packages based on water sports

* 28.8 per cent had packages associated with the Dubai Desert Classic (golf)

* 16.7 per cent had packages associated with the Dubai Rugby Sevens

* 12.5 per cent had packages in March for the Dubai World Cup (horse racing).

The DTCM now actively promotes Dubai as 'The Classic Golf Destination'. Dubai is home to the PGA Desert Classic and has several championship-standard grass courses that are open to visitors. Demand is so great that a central reservations office was created to manage bookings (www.dubaigolf.com). This is but one illustration of Dubai's well-deserved reputation for being the sporting capital of the Middle East. The calendar of events shown in Figure 3.11

EVENT AND TYPE	VENUE	DATE
Jet ski competition and races	Dubai Creek	Early August
Laser and sailing regatta	Dubai Creek	Early August
Traditional dhow sailing race (22 ft)	Dubai Creek	Early August
Emirates Grand Prix and Dubai Duty Free Grand Prix UIM Class One Offshore Power Boat Racing	Mina Seyahi	November
Dubai Rugby Sevens	Dubai Exiles Rugby Club	November/ early December
Eid camel races	Dubai Course	December
Dubai Marathon	To be announced	January
Dubai Tennis Open Men's & Women's	Dubai Tennis Stadium	February
Jebel Ali Hotel and Golf Resort Challenge Match	Jebel Ali Hotel & Golf Resort	February
Dubai Desert Classic Pro Am Tournament	Dubai Creek Golf & Yacht Club	March
Dubai Desert Classic	Emirates Golf Club	March
Dubai World Cup Races	Nad Al Sheba	March
Dubai–Muscat Sailing Race	Dubai Creek	March
UAE Marlboro Desert Challenge – Rally	Start at Hyatt Regency	November

Figure 3.11 Dubai's main sporting events

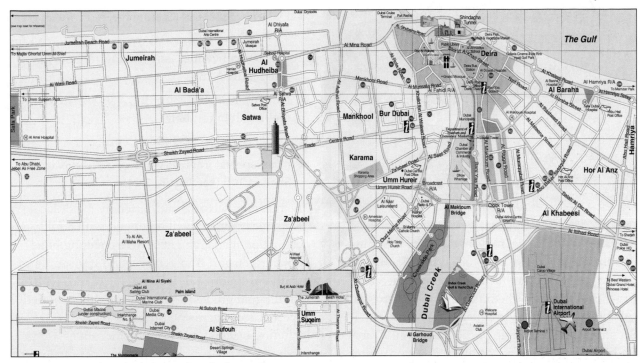

Figure 3.12 A detailed map of Dubai

attracts top personalities from all over the world and a varied programme of different sports helps Dubai to function as an all-year destination.

The variety of sports available is on a par with the best resorts in Europe and Asia, while there are others that are unique to the region. All the major hotels in Dubai boast very well-equipped sports centres. Visitors will find floodlit all-weather tennis, squash and badminton courts, swimming pools, snooker, table-tennis and fully equipped health and fitness centres at their disposal as part of their accommodation package.

Figure 3.12 shows features of central Dubai and it is possible to classify the built attractions in the following ways:

* shopping malls (e.g. Wafi City)

* traditional souks for gold and spices

* Dubai Museum and other historical buildings

* business tourism facilities (e.g. World Trade Centre)

* various luxury hotels in city-centre or beach locations.

A mixture of attractions and facilities

The concept of viewing a destination as an amalgam, with a combination of visitor attractions and facilities, is very appropriate in Dubai's case.

Figure 3.13 The lobby of Emirates Tower

The important aspect to be aware of is that the destination combines different types of attraction with a range of other facilities in a planned and organised manner. The mixing of the leisure and business tourism environments within Dubai illustrates this principle particularly well. Dubai is well established as the leading exhibition centre in the Middle East and it was recently voted the world's best conference venue. The city combines the facilities and services of one of the world's major international business centres with all the attractions of a top destination. This means that organisers and delegates alike can count on effective and successful events staged in a luxurious environment offering an outstanding range of recreational opportunities. The city now hosts more than 60 major exhibitions annually as well as numerous conferences, seminars, in-house corporate meetings and the like. This demand is serviced by a range of business facilities, including:

* Dubai Chamber of Commerce and Industry conference venue

* major hotel venues, such as Emirates Towers (see Figure 3.13)

* Dubai World Trade Centre, a 36 000 square metre exhibition hall

* Dubai Airport Exhibition Centre

* other special interest venues, such as Nad Al Sheba Club (see Figure 3.14).

The business sector is supported by major local companies that are well-equipped with a full destination management service covering hotel bookings, airport transfers, ground transport and a daily programme of tours and activities with multilingual guides. They also offer the required expertise for organising business-related travel, including original and exciting incentive programmes. The recent expansion of both leisure and business travel to Dubai has been matched by the growth in local inbound tour operations.

There is clear evidence to support the view that business and leisure tourism in Dubai have developed in parallel. Dubai's initial commercial development saw it rapidly become the leading port, trading centre and exhibition centre for the whole Gulf region. The city thus had the basic tourism infrastructure of hotels and travel-related services from the early 1990s, and these proved to be a very good starting point on which to build the leisure tourism product of the last decade. The DTCM markets Dubai as a destination for both leisure and business.

Figure 3.14 Nad Al Sheba racecourse

Assess the appeal of Dubai as a destination to each of the following UK visitor types: (a) a family with children, (b) a middle-aged ('empty nest') couple, and (c) a conference delegate. This exercise will help you prepare for the requirements of Assessment Objective 2.

The Al Maha desert resort

It is generally accepted amongst most nations that approximately 8–10 per cent of their land area should be put aside for the conservation of their indigenous habitats. The function of such a policy is to ensure that the nation's historic environment is permanently retained as part of its heritage and that the diversity of fauna and flora within the nation is kept intact as a representative sample of the original habitat. It is intended that such conserved areas can function without disturbance or undue intervention from human elements.

Al Maha is the first ecotourism resort in the UAE. Dubai has several environments worthy of conservation within such a framework. Apart from the dune environment at Al Maha there is also the mountain habitat around Hatta and the coast's intertidal strip. Each of these represents a separate, distinct and unique habitat type within Dubai. Each has its own fauna and flora, its own appeal to the visitor and its distinct historic, geological and archaeological merits. Al Maha has been developed with key ecotourism principles underpinning its commercial success.

As indicated on Figure 3.15, the environment must be free of intrusive disturbances which devalue the guests' experience of the surroundings. This includes the restriction of all artificial noise from the operation and ambient noise from the resort's surroundings. The restriction of any human structures which impinge on the natural landscape confines the development of the resort's own infrastructure to a minimum land area. The land making up the resort must provide a natural, original and unique environment for the guests, where they feel a part of the conservation process. This allows the guests to feel that their support is directly contributing to the conservation of the area they are experiencing.

One of the major contributors to the success of

Figure 3.15 Al Maha dunes

ecotourism resorts worldwide is the fact that the guests enjoy *exclusivity*. The rate charged is a function of the exclusivity enjoyed and paid for by the guest. The undisturbed settings, the personal attention and service standards not achievable in large public facilities are the basis of high-yield 'ecotourism' products. The guest must be assured of privacy, discretion and an unobtrusive environment. The experience must also be meaningful to the visitor, providing aspects which are educational, comfortable and divergent from normal lifestyle – thus assuring the guest that time spent in the resort is an enhancement to his or her quality of life.

The resort must meet the perceptions and expectations of the guests with regard to:

* accommodation
* facilities
* architecture and design
* surroundings
* ambience.

To meet these criteria, Al Maha has adapted traditional historic aspects, with operational requirements, to meet the guests' perception and expectation of the desert and Arabian heritage. A portion of land surrounding the core area of the resort has been demarcated for protection, and all activities capable of devaluing the environment are restricted. Isolation has been reinforced by means of the introduction of animal-proof fencing which will allow the establishment of indigenous species in viable breeding numbers within a free-roaming setting. The programme has been very successful and guests are now issued with their own fauna and flora checklist guide to record the various species that they have seen. The variety of headings used provides a suitable illustration of how far the desert resort has now developed in terms of conservation:

* grass (e.g. herb, dune, basket and cat's tail)

* shrub (e.g. broombush, dye plant and milkwort)

* herb (e.g. callous leaf, palm lettuce and Arabian cotton)

* plant (e.g. crimson wort, spiny disk and dwarf pea plant)

* tree (e.g. salam, ghaf and sidr)

* mammal (e.g. sand gazelle, Arabian hare and jird)

* reptile (e.g. monitor lizard, sand skink and sand snake)

* birds (common and may be resident or migrant – 300 species recorded).

Dubai's tourism future

The DTCM has set an aggressive target of attracting 15 million tourists by the year 2010. Projections for the immediate future are summarised in Figure 3.16.

YEAR	DUBAI HOTEL GUESTS (MILLIONS)	DUBAI HOTEL BEDS (THOUSANDS)
2003	5.24	39.8
2004	6.08	48.2
2005	7.06	55.9
2006	8.19	64.8
2007	9.49	75.2
2008	11.01	87.2
2009	12.78	101.2
2010	15.00	117.3

Figure 3.16 Targets for Dubai's tourism future

Such targets are not over-ambitious. Expatriates and foreign visitors can enjoy a relaxed and pleasant lifestyle in Dubai. There is virtually no crime, apartments and villas are modern and spacious, and the climate will appeal to those who enjoy warm weather. There are many clubs and societies in Dubai. Freedom of worship is allowed for all religions. Foreign newspapers, magazines, films and videos are all available. Alcohol may be consumed in hotels and in licensed club premises. Women can drive and move about unaccompanied.

In 2002, freehold ownership for UAE nationals as well as expatriates in certain select property developments was introduced in Dubai and 25-year mortgage loans became available. Initially, focus was centred on The Palm, Dubai Marina, and other developments of Emaar Properties. The potential for visiting friends and relatives will thus be substantially increased.

The Palm has already been described as the 'Eighth Wonder of the World' and is the sort of project that some say could only have taken place in Dubai. It consists of two massive, artificial islands: The Palm Jumeirah and The Palm Jebel Ali. Each island is being built in the shape of a palm tree, consisting of a crown of seventeen fronds, a trunk, and a surrounding 'crescent island', the back of which forms a protective breakwater. Each island will be approximately 6 kilometres long and 5.5 kilometres wide. Together they will add nearly 120 kilometres of much-sought-after coastline to Dubai. Approximately 3000 homes and at least 40 luxury hotels will be built on each island, capable of berthing a total of 400 yachts. It is expected that the first residents will move into The Palm Jumeirah before the end of 2004. The Palm is just one of several Nakheel residential projects; others include The World, Jumeirah Islands, Jumeirah Lake Towers and The Gardens.

Dubai will continue to improve the destination's infrastructure, and the following are just some of the developments that are already planned and in actual construction or development to support visitor growth targets:

* Hydropolis – the world's first underwater hotel

* Dubai airport expansion to handle 70 million passengers by 2016

* Dubai Festival City – a 4 km site along the Creek
* Dubai Land – the region's biggest tourism project aiming for 200 000 visitors a day – to include five themed leisure areas and the Mall of Arabia, the world's biggest mall
* Dubai Railway project for 2008
* Burj Dubai – the world's tallest tower.

We next look at some other types of destination to see how and why they appeal to different types of visitor.

Destination: Barcelona

Almost 4.5 million people live in the Barcelona metropolitan area. The city enjoys a prime location, bathed by the sea and having excellent transport links with the rest of Europe. The Mediterranean and Europe are the defining characteristics of Catalonia.

Barcelona is a modern, cosmopolitan city, but has inherited many centuries of history. Its geographic location and the open character of its inhabitants are the reasons why the city is being culturally enriched all the time. It has a valuable architectural and monumental heritage – five of its buildings have been designated World Heritage Sites. The entire city guarantees that visitors will enjoy taking a stroll around its streets which generate a sophisticated charm.

Barcelona enjoys a Mediterranean climate, with mild winters and warm summers. It is a coastal city and has over four kilometres of urban beaches and large areas of nearby forest. Although it is a large city, it is easy to get around using public transport and on foot. Furthermore, you can reach any point in the city by metro, bus and taxi. Barcelona is the capital of Catalonia. Its inhabitants are open and welcoming. The people of Barcelona speak Catalan, their own language, and Spanish. Many of them also understand a little English and French.

Barcelona has importance as a visitor destination. In 1990 the total number of visitors just exceeded 7.2 million, and that figure had risen to nearly 8.7 million in 2002 – a 20 per cent increase. Furthermore, the city regularly attracts large numbers of visitors from the UK and Ireland (see Figure 3.17).

YEAR	VISITORS FROM UK AND IRELAND
1990	4.1%
1995	7.2%
2001	15.6%
2002	14.4%
2003	11.8%

Figure 3.17 Visitors to Barcelona from the UK and Ireland

There are several reasons for this impressive recent growth and significant appeal to the UK market. A key factor is that 80 per cent of visitor arrivals come by plane and this has resulted in Barcelona becoming the world's 36th busiest airport, handling over 22 million passengers in 2003. Barcelona is now served with many low-cost flights from the UK, and airports providing services to the city include:

* Aberdeen
* Birmingham
* Bristol
* East Midlands
* Edinburgh
* Gatwick
* Glasgow
* Prestwick
* Leeds/Bradford
* Liverpool
* Luton
* Newcastle
* Stansted.

This means that Barcelona is a very accessible destination for UK visitors.

We have already seen that the city generates media attention and that it contains a range of affordable options. However, what other attractions does the city contain and why does it appear to be increasingly popular with visitors? The results of various surveys by the local tourist board indicate a high degree of visitor approval for the following aspects of Barcelona's total tourism product:

* architecture and culture
* leisure and entertainment
* shopping, restaurants and hotels
* character of the local people
* public transport
* value for money of restaurants

* value for money of shopping
* value for money of hotels
* access to Barcelona
* signs and information
* safety in the city

* general cleanliness
* low atmospheric pollution and low noise.

Figure 3.18 shows that there are a range of visitor attractions in the city and that six locations attract over a million visitors.

Ajuntament de Barcelona

E S T A D I S

Statistics > Statistical yearbook of Barcelona city. 2004 > Tourism

4. Other tourist information

4.1. Visitors to places of interest. 1999-2003

Lugares de interés	1999	2000	2001	2002	2003
Museos y equipamientos culturales					
Sagrada Família	1.222.497	1.420.087	1.554.529	2.024.091	2.056.458
Centre Cultural "Caixa de Catalunya" (1)	1.322.584	1.386.721	1.212.190	1.391.274	1.405.426
Centre Cultural i Social de la Fundació "La Caixa" (2)	322.550	344.097	234.422	1.296.831	1.133.220
Museu F.C. Barcelona President Núñez	1.154.604	1.156.090	1.161.038	1.168.053	1.032.763
Museu Picasso	1.081.843	1.026.549	1.109.356	1.027.836	887.958 (4)
Fundació Joan Miró	474.810	497.295	492.457	493.343	524.621
Museu Nacional d'Art Catalunya (MNAC)	347.884	368.063	442.770	433.108	445.701
Centre de Cultura Contemporània (CCCB)	150.878	136.290	188.115	160.128	162.954
Museu d'Història de Catalunya	161.138	170.075	190.475	302.326	336.453
Museu d'Història de la Ciutat	200.277	172.421	183.707	242.682	170.325
Museu d'Art Contemporani (MACBA)	150.722	173.098	192.351	236.235	317.050
Fundació Arqueològica Clos	21.856	170.340	220.614	221.701	301.579
Museu de Cera	206.517	189.265	187.354	190.202	192.993
Museu Marítim	174.065	249.830	193.019	180.110	257.352
Museu de la Ciència	260.722	262.561	241.081	135.677 (3)	-
Museu Militar	103.856	96.329	93.831	114.275	130.614
Museu de Ceràmica i de les Arts Decoratives	115.412	152.339	148.777	107.567	114.625
Museu de Ciències Naturals (Geologia i Zoologia)	49.075	61.501	64.597	81.510	105.343
Museu d'Art Modern (MNAC)	97.891	101.811	62.534	73.245	66.979
Fundació Antoni Tàpies	67.899	79.783	71.312	66.423	69.056
Museu Monestir Pedralbes	60.931	57.201	64.668	63.636	59.096
F. Thyssen / Bornemisza	46.939	48.106	55.658	55.048	49.212
Museu de l'Eròtica	44.555	44.638	29.602	45.596	37.202
Museu Tèxtil Indumentària	25.456	71.074	30.367	30.973	31.253
Museu Frederic Marès	18.894	23.470	23.620	24.844	31.414
Equipamientos lúdicos					
L'Aquàrium	1.588.050	1.563.493	1.527.283	1.450.385	-
Poble Espanyol de Montjuïc	1.347.310	1.478.546	1.429.378	1.446.246	-
Parc Zoològic	893.000	930.000	958.474	992.173	1.015.000
Imax	1.163.095	818.707	603.282	694.038	-
Parc d'Atraccions Tibidabo	464.623	405.231	410.010	407.459	-
Parc del Laberint	134.000	127.129	144.946	144.065	141.841
Mirador de Colom	77.799	103.500	102.225	122.116	127.162
Transportes					
Barcelona Bus Turístic	1.648.467	2.650.833	2.950.392	3.493.923	3.750.771
Telefèric Montjuïc	391.208	444.899	444.802	498.949	584.771
Funicular Montjuïc	385.014	420.647	364.503	120.792	-
Golondrinas	206.526	290.232	187.590	237.882	-
Tramvia Blau	181.502	198.908	215.773	228.373	239.800

(1) Espai Gaudí & la Pedrera.
(2) Abierto el febrero de 02 (nueva sede).
(3) Cerrado por reformas des de julio de 02.
(4) Cerrado del 25 de febrero al 10 de abril 2003 por reinstalación de las piezas de la colección permanente en las nuevas salas recientemente remodeladas.

Departament d'Estadística. Ajuntament de Barcelona.
Fuente: Institut de Cultura. Ajuntament de Barcelona.

Figure 3.18 Tourist information for Barcelona

Research a selection of the attractions listed in Figure 3.18. Explain their relative visitor appeal. This exercise will help you generate evidence for Assessment Objective 3.

Barcelona is also popular because it is only an hour away from the purpose-built resort of Universal Mediterranea (see Figure 3.19). This giant theme park, which opened in 1994, attracts thousands of holidaymakers every year who journey through its five worlds (Mediterránia, Far West, Mexico, Polynesia and China) on its many rides and attractions.

Enjoying an enviable coastal location, between Salou and Vila-seca on Spain's Costa Dorada, this 117-hectare site boasts entertainment aimed at all age groups. There are nightly shows, including Fiestaventura in the Mediterranean world, as well as many other attractions, including the Sea Odyssey underwater adventure, the Stampida rollercoaster ride, and the Grand Canyon Rapids and Tutuki Splash water rides. Templo del Fuego, which opened in 2001, has the greatest number of fire and water effects ever used in any attraction, while the big attraction for the 2002 season was the new Costa Caribe Caribbean-themed water park. Visitors who wish to spend a few days in the park can stay in one of the many hotels on site, all of which share a beach area, Playa Larga, where guests can relax and soak up the Mediterranean sun. The park is owned by the Universal Studios Recreation Group, responsible for other theme parks around the world, including Universal Orlando and Universal Studios Hollywood.

Research the facilities, products and services provided by the hotels in this purpose-built resort and compare them with Emirates Towers hotel in Dubai.

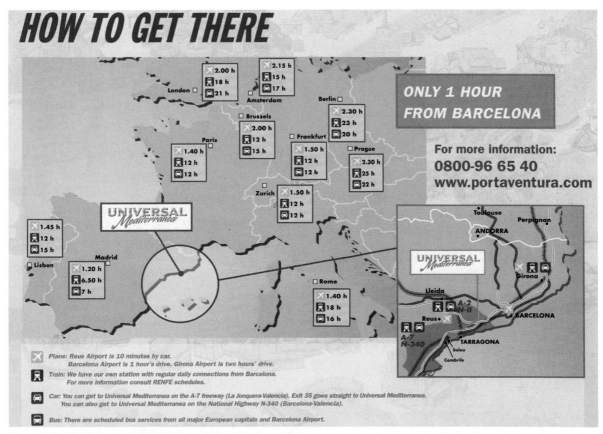

Figure 3.19 Universal Mediterranea near Barcelona

Destination: Southport

Southport has been recognised as a leading British seaside resort for many years. It is also famous for the internationally acclaimed Lord Street, a mile-long boulevard renowned for the quality of its shopping – along one side are shops with Victorian glass-topped canopies and on the opposite side are gardens, fountains and classical buildings.

There are miles of golden sands on the beach for holidaymakers to enjoy as well as excellent resort facilities such as a pier, baths, bowling greens, amusement park, marine lake, civic theatres, arts centre and art gallery.

The town was founded in 1792 when William Sutton opened a hotel and the name 'South-port' first appeared in proper use during the year 1798. Following a pattern common to all UK seaside resorts, the first major development was in 1848 when a rail service became available from Liverpool to the town (visitors travelled previously by canal and road). Then, from 1853, people could go by train to the resort from Manchester (via Wigan), and the seaside town attracted thousands of workers from the Lancashire mill towns.

The Victorian era left the town with a glorious legacy:

* its spaciousness
* the parks, gardens and wide tree-lined streets
* Lord Street, one of Britain's finest boulevards.

The town grew and developed as a traditional UK seaside resort. Now it shows many of the features that characterise such destinations. However, the following statistics show that tourism is still of great local significance:

* 5.1 million visitors per annum
* 550 000 staying visitors generating £65 million
* 4.6 million day visitors generating £119.4 million
* 86 hotels (about 2300 bedrooms)
* 1.6 million bed–nights
* employment for over 6700 permanent staff and about 5000 seasonal jobs.

The destination's tourism profile can be summarised as follows:

* main visitor origin regions – Merseyside, Cheshire, Manchester, Lancashire, West Yorkshire, Scotland, North Yorkshire and Staffordshire
* key markets – short breaks, conferences, festival and events, day-trip and group travel, golf, birdwatching, and walking/cycling.

Southport's reputation as England's golfing capital is well deserved. The resort is home to a number of premier links and parkland courses including Royal Birkdale, Formby, Hesketh, Hillside, Southport and Ainsdale, and Formby Hall Golf Club. Many have hosted top tournaments such as the Ryder Cup and the Curtis Cup. Royal Birkdale will host the Open Championships for the ninth time in 2008. With Royal Liverpool and Royal Lytham St Annes situated close by, the region is increasingly being recognised as a golfer's paradise.

Visitors are also attracted to a variety of events held in the Southport area each year. The following examples of visitor numbers illustrate different aspects of the destination's appeal:

* British Lawnmower Museum – 5000
* Southport British Musical Firework Championship – 45 000
* Southport Air Show – 230 000
* Southport Christmas Festival – 25 000
* Festival of Street Entertainment – 12 000
* Southport Flower Show – 120 000
* Southport Zoo – 58 000
* Southport Pleasureland – 2.6 million
* Southport Jazz Festival – 30 000
* Southport Pier – 250 000
* Summer Classics – 4500.

Theory into practice

Research a selection of these events and assess their relative appeal to different visitor groups.

Southport Pier, located on the seafront (see Figure 3.20), reopened in 2002 following a £7 million restoration programme. The pier, second longest in the UK, has proved to be popular with visitors, with well in excess of half a million people having taken a stroll along this unique attraction since it was redeveloped. The views at pier-end are truly panoramic. The beautifully designed Pier Pavilion is very popular with visitors. It houses a number of traditional style amusements – a throwback to Southport's golden era – plus an exhibition tracking the history of the pier itself. This is a specialised attraction for 'pier buffs', who are a significant special-interest group. The pier also regularly hosts a number of visitor events – a recent Pier Extravaganza event proved to be a huge success.

Recent investment in the development of Southport's Theatre and Floral Hall Complex has boosted the number and quality of conferences to the town and highlighted the need for further quality accommodation to serve the conference market. The complex is Merseyside's largest and most flexible multi-purpose venue, providing clients with full technical support, in-house catering and professional coordination. The complex is conveniently located on Southport's Promenade just a short walk from the town's wide range of accommodation, dining and leisure facilities.

The traditional tiered theatre auditorium has an impressive 1631 capacity which can be conveniently reduced for smaller numbers of 250. There are large roller shutter doors to the stage for ease of unloading and access. The 141 square metre stage with technical facilities can accommodate up to three vehicles, making it ideal for car and product launches. The spacious foyer area with its own amenities links the theatre to the magnificent Floral Hall ballroom. This can host an array of events such as conferences, seminars and dinners for 150 to 1200 guests, as well as exhibitions and trade shows with 850 square metres of floor space and a 100 square metre integral stage. The Floral Hall has the flexibility to be transformed to suit individual customer needs

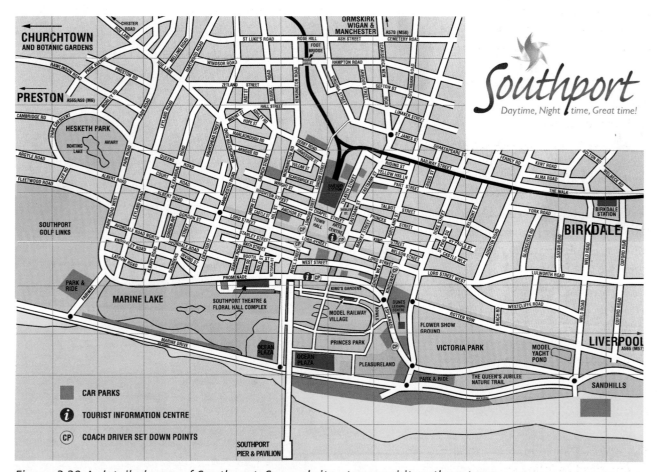

Figure 3.20 A detailed map of Southport. See website at www.visitsouthport.com

with in-house catering, technical and bar facilities. Five smaller suites complement the larger facilities and are ideal for more intimate events – seminars, weddings, private functions or receptions for up to 250 guests. There is on-site parking for up to 200 vehicles and level access to all suites for patrons with disabilities.

Environmentally, there have been significant strides over recent years, particularly the new £9 million sea wall and the general landscaping and enhancing of the facilities on the promenade and seafront, including some innovative sculptures. The Victorian architecture of the town has been preserved and enhanced. Outstanding and well-maintained gardens and open spaces have advanced the town's reputation as an attractive floral resort. The internationally renowned Southport Flower Show is thriving and moves from one successful event to another.

Southport is a major retail and shopping destination. Park-and-ride schemes have been introduced to improve visitor movements around the resort. Many new restaurants, bars and cafés have opened up and many have been refurbished. The resort has a lively atmosphere by day and by night. The nightlife is excellent, with a wide choice of clubs and musical tastes. Pleasureland, the theme park, is Southport's biggest attraction, with over 2.6 million visitors each year. After many years a £11 million scheme including a new rollercoaster, the 'Traumatizer', and a new family entertainment centre, 'Casablanca', including a bowling alley, amusement arcade, bar and restaurant has been developed, along with landscaping improvements in the theme park. Events continue to play a major role in attracting visitors to the area.

Southport has a varied tourism product and it is no surprise that its Tourist Information Service receives over 44 000 phone calls a year and 246 000 walk-in visitors. The resort's main website, www.visitsouthport.com, receives half a million hits each year.

Theory into practice

Use Figure 3.20 and your own research to explain why Southport attracts both leisure and business visitors.

Destination: Keswick and the Northern Lakes

Lake District National Park is the largest (230 000 hectares), most spectacular and most visited of Britain's national parks. It regularly has around 20 million visitors a year. The park was established by Parliament in 1951 with two principal aims:

* to conserve and enhance the natural beauty, wildlife and cultural heritage of the national park
* to promote opportunities for the understanding and enjoyment of the special qualities of the national park by the public.

The park as a whole contains many features that may attract different types of visitor. It has several unique selling points, such as:

* complex geology
* diverse landscape of the Lakeland fells
* the largest concentration of common land in Britain
* traditional livestock breeds like Herdwick sheep
* varied habitats, especially freshwater ones
* extensive semi-natural woodland
* the highest concentration of outdoor activity centres in the UK
* one of the most diverse range of tourist facilities, attractions and accommodation in the country
* internationally important archaeological sites
* distinctive settlement character
* its own dialects and distinctive sports such as hound trailing, fell running, and Cumberland and Westmorland wrestling.

Visitors flock to the area to take advantage of the peaceful scenery, the wildlife, the many good walks and the opportunities to take part in adventure tourism activities.

Theory into practice

Study Figures 3.21 and 3.22. List the various outdoor activities that different visitor types could undertake in both locations. This exercise can help you generate evidence for Assessment Objective 4.

Figure 3.21 A view of the tranquillity of the Lake District

Figure 3.22 A visitor activity location in the Lake District

Keswick retains the attractive appearance of a traditional small market town, the weekly stalls still set around the Moot market hall which dominates the town centre. The Tourist Information Centre is conveniently placed in this fine old listed building.

Despite its small size, Keswick's popularity as a visitor destination means that it contains a variety of indoor and outdoor attractions far wider than you might expect. Three very individual museums, a highly successful theatre, the cinema and art and craft exhibitions are balanced, for the very active, by the leisure pool, indoor climbing centre and the sports hall.

Figure 3.23 illustrates the appeal of the Keswick area to a variety of tourists. The map shows a range of both natural and built attractions. Some are quite specialised. Located in the Borrowdale valley near Grange, at the southern end of Derwentwater (www.lakelandscape.co.uk/derwentwater.htm), the Bowder Stone is one of Lakeland's most famous landmarks. The huge boulder weighs around 2000 tonnes, is 9 metres (30 feet) high and lies balanced precariously on its corner. It has become a local attraction for rock climbers and is visited on a regular basis throughout the year. A sturdy wooden ladder allows visitors to climb on top of the stone and it acts as a minor viewpoint. Educational groups will visit the site to conduct field investigations into footpath erosion and undertake assessment of the impacts of tourism within a national park.

Theory into practice

Study Figure 3.23 on the next page and identify the variety of both natural and artificial attractions to be found in the Keswick area. Research their appeal to different visitor groups. This exercise will help you generate evidence for Assessment Objectives 2 and 3.

The national park contains many facilities that attract student groups. Near the village of Threlkeld is the Blencathra Field Centre (see Figure 3.24), one of the properties run by the Field Studies Council (FSC). The FSC's mission statement is 'Environmental Understanding for All', and we can now look at some of the ways in which this has been put into practice.

The Blencathra Field Centre is owned by Lake District National Park but is managed by the Field Studies Council which is an educational charity. The centre was opened in 1994 and delivers part of the National Park Education Service. The centre provides residential courses for groups aged between 8 and 80 as well as

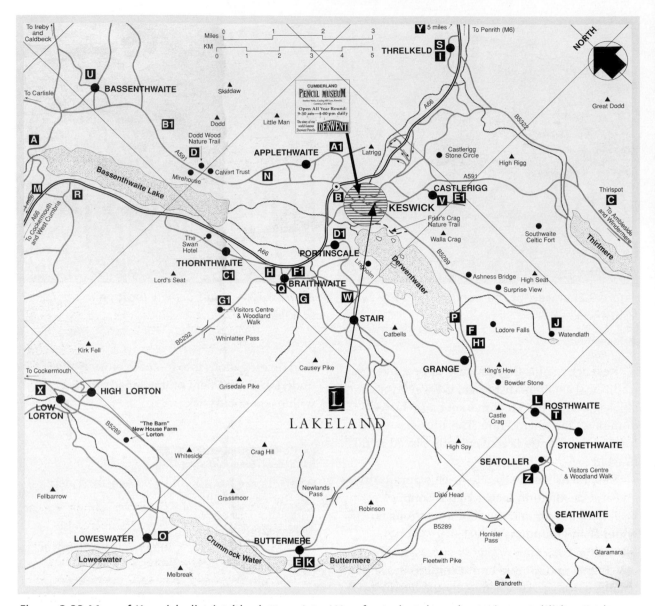

Figure 3.23 Map of Keswick district (the letters A to H1 refer to hotels and catering establishments).

providing a residential base for independent groups who wish to take advantage of this quiet location four miles from Keswick. The centre also has three self-catering cottages which are of three Cumbria Tourist Board Keys standard. It delivers courses for over 3000 people each year, with typical stays anything between two and seven nights. Depending on the season, there can be up to 100 visitors on site each night. It is not open to the casual bed-and-breakfast visitor market.

Traditionally, the main role of FSC centres was to provide courses for educational groups, especially for schools on a field trip. Blencathra, which is also an eco-centre, now finds itself frequently hosting courses for diverse outside groups. For these customers the main requirements are the accommodation, catering, specialist tutoring, and a high standard of customer care available at the centre. The centre has clearly adapted to customer needs and wants and it is now appealing to a much wider client

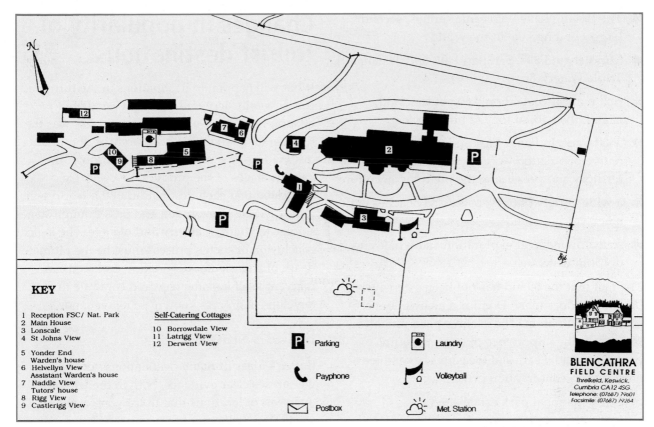

KEY

1	Reception FSC/ Nat. Park	**Self-Catering Cottages**
2	Main House	
3	Lonscale	10 Borrowdale View
4	St Johns View	11 Latrigg View
		12 Derwent View
5	Yonder End
	Warden's house
6	Helvellyn View
	Assistant Warden's house
7	Naddle View
	Tutors' house
8	Rigg View
9	Castlerigg View

P Parking

📞 Payphone

✉ Postbox

🖥 Laundry

🚩 Volleyball

🌤 Met. Station

**BLENCATHRA
FIELD CENTRE**
Threlkeld, Keswick,
Cumbria CA12 4SG.
Telephone: (07687) 79601
Facsimile: (07687) 79264

Figure 3.24 The Blencathra Centre in the national park

base than it did in the past. Bookings are conducted on a one-to-one basis and individual requirements are given every attention. This has resulted in a customer base that is far more mixed than just school groups doing a coursework project visit. Even at this small scale, the significance of both leisure and business visitor requirements is very evident.

Theory into practice

Research the types of courses available at an FSC centre. Suggest reasons why Blencathra near Keswick would be a good location to deliver such products and services.

We shall end our destination case studies with an example from the tropics and briefly examine the visitor appeal of an unspoilt Caribbean island. Such a location has many attractions for the adventurous twenty-first century tourist.

Destination: Dominica

The Caribbean island of Dominica, shown earlier in Figure 3.5 on page 97, was discovered by Columbus in 1493. The island is situated towards the northern end of the Lesser Antilles, lying between the two French islands of Guadeloupe to the north and Martinique to the south. The island is 47 km long and 26 km wide. It is volcanic in origin and ruggedly beautiful, with towering green mountains covered with dense tropical forests, deep valleys and countless streams providing magnificent scenic views. Dominica's physical features are unique selling points that help to set it apart from other Caribbean island destinations.

Dominica now markets itself as 'The nature island of the Caribbean' and as 'The Caribbean's ultimate Eco-destination'. Visitors are attracted to the island to experience a range of natural wonders, including:

✱ Morne Trois Pitons National Park – UNESCO Natural World Heritage Site

✱ Valley of Desolation

* The Boiling Lake – volcanic springs, second largest boiling lake in the world

* Middleham Falls, Sari Sari Falls and Trafalgar Triple Waterfalls

* rich natural vegetation – 60 per cent of the island, the habitat for 172 bird species

* 3500 Carib Indians – descendants of the first native population – occupying their own territory and preserving the pre-colonial culture

* a wide variety of bays, coves and beaches with black volcanic sand

* scuba diving, reef exploration and whale and dolphin watching.

The fact that the island has not been extensively developed does make Dominica an excellent eco-tourism destination. The island's government recognises the importance of environmental protection and a series of measures have given emphasis to conservation principles:

* 1975 – national park established

* 1987 – Cabrits Historical Park established

* spear fishing prohibited

* removal of living sea organisms and artefacts from wrecks not allowed

* ecological resorts established (e.g. Papillote Wilderness Retreat).

The island is now becoming an established Caribbean destination because of the quality of its managed physical environment. The strategy has clearly worked and annual visitor arrivals have increased from 47 000 to more than 63 000 over recent years. It has become a niche destination and attracts a specialised market segment.

However, Dominica has certain seasonal disadvantages because of its tropical location. Each of the Earth's major climatic zones may contain natural hazards, depending on the time of year, which visitors will have to make allowance for. In this case it is the risk of late summer hurricanes that bring an annual threat to the tourism economies of the Caribbean and Florida. Dominica was hit by particularly violent storms in 1979, 1980 and 1999. The risk of such tropical storms explains why July, August and September are 'low season' in such destinations.

Changes in popularity of tourist destinations

What will happen to destinations in the future? It is generally accepted that the Canadian geographer R. W. Butler, writing in 1980, was the first person to liken the development of tourist destinations to a product passing through the various stages of the product life-cycle. He suggested that each destination in the world will follow a cycle of evolution and pass through stages similar to youth, maturity and old age. The logical conclusion of such a process must be the ultimate death of a particular destination, unless it can reinvent itself in some way and continue to develop – a process known as 'rejuvenation'.

Butler's stages

Butler's ideas fit many destinations very well and we can see clear evidence, both in the UK and overseas, of locations that fit into one of the six stages of development that he proposed.

1: Exploration stage
A small number of tourists make their own travel arrangements. Only a few visitors come to the country, maybe backpackers or some other type of independent traveller. There are no charter flights or tourist services and the cost to the traveller, both in time and/or money, can be high. No investment in tourist infrastructure has been made at this stage. However, the economic, social, cultural and environmental impacts caused by tourism will be virtually nil.

2: Involvement
Some local residents begin to provide facilities exclusively for the use of visitors. Visitor numbers increase and local businesses start providing services. The local population has accepted the arrival of visitors and the destination starts to grow, with locals actually becoming involved with promotional activities.

3: Development
Local suppliers and providers of tourism products and services become increasingly involved in the development process. The area becomes established as a tourist destination with a defined market. As

the visitors keep coming, more businesses enter the market which is now becoming profitable. Package holidays begin and the destination sees marked expansion with the arrival of foreign operators and investors. As the country becomes more popular and the infrastructure begins to take shape, more tour operators become interested and organise package tours to the country. A range of brochures become available at travel agents, advertisements appear in the media. Competition between businesses is growing, so prices start to fall and so do profit margins. With increased competition resulting in falling prices, different type of customers will now be able to visit the destination. This reflects a well-defined tourist destination shaped by heavy marketing in tourist-generating regions.

4: Consolidation

Tourism now starts to dominate the economic base of the area and starts to have an adverse effect on the traditional economy and lifestyle. Local agricultural land is given over to resort development but there is not a proportional increase in local wealth, per capita income or job creation. The rate of increase in numbers of visitors will have started to decline, although total numbers will still increase.

5: Stagnation

Peak numbers of visitors will have been reached. There is a growing awareness of negative environmental, social, cultural and economic tourism impacts. Sales go down as the country goes out of fashion and there is evidence that the original cultural and natural attractiveness of the destination has been lost. Profits are low, businesses may leave the market or diversify to other types of product. Furthermore, because there may be fewer businesses in the local tourism marketplace, prices can be increased, thus accelerating the decline.

6: Decline versus rejuvenation

Butler's model of destination development and evolution ends with a series of options that all resorts will have to face at some time. Figure 3.25 shows the following:

✱ Immediate decline (a) – Visitor numbers fall quite rapidly and the tourism base severely contracts, resulting in a local economic depression.

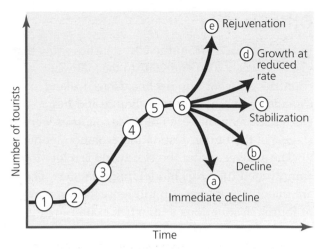

Figure 3.25 An illustration of Butler's six stages and the possible future trend

✱ Decline (b) – The destination will face a declining market and will be unable to compete with newer destinations or destinations which better meet the needs of the modern tourist.

✱ Stabilization (c) – The destination is able to maintain its market share but there is little, if any, continued growth and development.

✱ Growth at reduced rate (d) – The effects of competition mean that even with new development plans, the destination is never able to return to the levels of previous growth and development.

✱ Rejuvenation (e) – If major changes are made, such as improving the environment and tourism infrastructure, better marketing or the addition of more attractions for example, then the destination may experience a period of rejuvenation. This is a period of further growth and development brought about by innovation and renewed diversification. In effect, the destination reinvents itself and extends its appeal to different market segments.

Assessment activity

Identify locations in the world that would fit into each of these stages of destination evolution, giving reasons for your choices.

To help you with this task, consider the five destination studies that we have looked at and decide where they should be placed within the model. Some destinations, because of their long history, will have passed through several stages.

Other factors

In terms of travel from the UK, statistics show that visits between 2000 and 2002 to the following countries all went into decline: Israel, Iceland, Canada, the USA, Germany, France and India. Does this mean that each of these countries were at stage 6 of the Butler destination evolution model?

The answer is that the real world is a lot more complicated than this model might suggest. There are many factors that can influence the popularity of tourist destinations and, when examining the appeal of any one particular location, you have to be aware of wider issues and the conditions operating elsewhere.

We shall now examine how certain factors can work together to influence the popularity of certain destinations.

Visits to the USA by UK tourists would have been badly affected during the years 2000 to 2002 by a number of circumstances. The following list of figures relating to New York City international visitors from 1998 clearly shows the effect of the terrorist attacks on 11 September 2001:

* 1998 – 6.0 million
* 1999 – 6.6 million
* 2000 – 6.8 million
* **2001** – 5.7 million
* 2002 – 5.1 million
* 2003 – 4.8 million
* 2004 – 5.1 million

From the UK's point of view, 870 000 tourists visited New York City, still down on the million plus that went in year 2000. Fear of terrorist attacks may be only one factor that explains this drop. The weakness of the pound sterling against the US dollar was also a significant factor in that it made the USA a comparatively expensive destination to visit. However, 2004 saw a reversal with the pound strengthening against the dollar,

thus making the USA much more affordable for the UK outbound tourist. The major transatlantic carriers are always quick to maintain their flight volumes, and so cheap airfares to the USA (to New York in particular) are frequently available.

Therefore, in just a two-year period, UK residents travelling to New York will have been influenced by both *economic* and *political* influences. It was pointed out at the start of the chapter that individuals can form incorrect perceptions about particular destinations. Let us now try to identify current world destinations where particular factors and circumstances are influencing the number of visitors that are received.

Bulgaria is a very cost-effective destination for the UK visitor. It remains outside of the European Union and prices are low. The Black Sea coastal resorts around Varna attracted over 100 000 Britons in 2004, and with companies offering value packages for 2005 the trend looks set to continue. Some current packages are shown in Figure 3.26.

TOUR OPERATOR	PACKAGE HOLIDAY DETAILS
Balkan Holidays	Fourteen nights bed & breakfast at the Hotel Varshava in Golden Sands Prices start at £199 including flights
Airtours	Seven nights all-inclusive at the Grand Hotel in Sunny Beach Prices start at £339 including flights
Cosmos	Seven nights bed & breakfast at the Hotel Strandja in Sunny Beach Prices start at £319 including flights

Figure 3.26 Sample holiday packages to Bulgaria in 2004

The mass-market operators are now promoting the destination and the main resorts have clear appeal to both families and budget-conscious travellers. Charter flights into Bourgas and Varna airports mean that Bulgaria has the potential to rival Spain in terms of being a UK visitor destination.

Spain's Costa Brava was once at the forefront of mass tourism and during the 1970s was the leading destination for UK holidaymakers. However, in 2004, tour operators Cosmos and First Choice announced they were axing the destination from their 2005 holiday programmes. The resort has become a victim of its past success and is suffering from a combination of over-commercialisation, negative media coverage, rising costs and a dated image. In terms of the model of destination evolution, the Costa Brava is clearly at stage 6. Decline seems likely, but the Spanish Tourist Board hopes that the destination can be rejuvenated. The tourist board is now planning to market the Costa Brava as more than just a beach resort. It will now include the local region's countryside and culture in its marketing literature and will refer to the destination as Costa Brava Pirineu de Girona. It remains to be seen whether or not this rebranding will influence the UK travelling public.

The present UK leisure travel market is in a state of change. The summer of 2004 saw an 8 per cent drop in mass market sales. Many analysts put this down to rising UK interest rates rather than fears over the Iraq conflict or the threat of SARS infection. However, industry forecasts suggest that mass-market sales will show a further decline in 2005. This suggests that UK leisure travel consumer behaviour is altering, a development that will have a significant effect on destinations. Current UK leisure travel market research indicates the following:

✱ Forty-five per cent have taken at least four holidays in the past two years.

✱ Thirty-one per cent have bought a holiday through a travel agent.

✱ Thirty-two per cent have booked on-line.

✱ Thirty-eight per cent are likely to use a travel agent in the future.

✱ Thirty-six per cent are likely to use the Internet in the future.

This research suggests that the UK travelling public will become more independent and further shy away from the traditional mass-market product. Short breaks will continue to grow in popularity, which will favour established destinations such as Barcelona.

There are bound to be winners and losers amongst the various long- and short-haul destinations that are currently visited by UK tourists. Some destinations will continue to benefit from the positive impacts of tourism development, whereas others will suffer negative effects. Some examples of the key issues involved in tourist/host encounters within destinations are shown in Figure 3.27.

Positive aspects, such as
Increased employment opportunities
Preservation of traditional culture, folklore, festivals
Better recreational facilities
Better infrastructure
Negative aspects, such as
Decline in traditional employment
Population migration
Seasonal underemployment
Exposure to alternative lifestyle(s)
Increased crime
Decline in importance of traditional way of life.

Figure 3.27 Key issues in encounters within destinations

Environmental impacts of tourism within destinations can exert positive effects such as:

✱ conservation of heritage sites

✱ regeneration and redevelopment of derelict sites

✱ pollution controls

✱ traffic management schemes etc.

However, continued tourism development can equally result in negative effects such as:

✱ urban sprawl

✱ traffic congestion

✱ over-development at 'honeypot' sites

✱ footpath erosion and landscape degradation

✱ loss of open spaces

✱ water supply issues

✱ wildlife habitat disruption

✱ loss of bio-diversity

✱ water and air pollution.

Such issues will be viewed by potential visitors in terms of their own personal expectations, needs and wants. Many factors influence an individual's decision to visit a particular destination, as was indicated earlier in Figure 3.3. It remains to be seen how the travelling public will view the great variety of destinations that now actively compete for their custom.

Theory into practice

Make a copy of the following table and add as many correct illustrations as you can for each category, indicating the effect on UK visitor numbers. Some examples have been provided to start you off.

FACTOR	UK DESTINATIONS	SHORT-HAUL DESTINATIONS	LONG-HAUL DESTINATIONS
Cost of accommodation	Weekend offers		
Cost of transport		easyJet budget flights	Competition to key gateways (e.g. NYC)
Costs at destination	Remote areas		High value of sterling against many currencies
Tour operator promotional activity		Thomson's summer sale offers	
Destination promotional activity			Dubai DTCM
Over-commercialisation		Benidorm and other resorts	Niagara Falls
Crime and social problems	Nottingham city-centre drinkers	Rome thefts	Jamaica
Political instability/unrest		Gibraltar	
Terrorism		Basque Spain	Post-9/11 NYC
Positive media coverage			Dubai
Negative media coverage			
Positive tourism management	Lake District National Park Authority		
Negative tourism management			
Growth in independent travel		Timeshares and property in Spain	
Growth in short breaks			
Exclusivity		La Manga	Al Maha
Increased accessibility		easyJet new routes	Emirates direct flights from LHR, LGW, BHX, MAN & GLA
Water hazard	Cornwall floods		
Air hazard			Los Angeles smog
Noise pollution			
Natural disasters	Foot and mouth outbreak	Ski resort avalanches	Caribbean hurricanes

NYC = New York City; LHR = Heathrow; LGW = Gatwick; BHX = Birmingham; MAN = Manchester; GLA = Glasgow

The tsunami in south-east Asia

We end this study of travel destinations with a review of the effects of the terrible disaster that struck south-east Asia at the end of 2004.

On 26 December, at 0758 local time, an earthquake of magnitude 9 occurred off the west coast of northern Sumatra, Indonesia. This was the fourth largest earthquake in the world since 1900. The earthquake generated a tsunami (tidal wave) which swept across the Indian Ocean within hours of the event and brought devastation to a large number of coastal areas, including several important tourist destinations. The main areas affected by the tsunami are shown on Figure 3.28.

Over 280 000 people are thought to have lost their lives in this natural disaster. The overall local impacts caused by the wave were very variable, but Figure 3.29 identifies key aspects of the scale of the disaster.

Figure 3.28 Some of the main areas affected by the tsunami

COUNTRY	DEAD/MISSING	HOMELESS	DESTRUCTION
Indonesia	220 000	517 000	1550 villages
Sri Lanka	36 000	835 000	88 000 homes
India	15 700	627 100	157 400 homes
Thailand	9 000	8 500	Coastal resorts

Figure 3.29 Some provisional estimates of the human impact of the tsunami of 26 December 2004

Furthermore, a large number of European visitors to the above destinations were also victims of the disaster. Interim figures of casualties for the UK, Germany and Sweden are summarised in Figure 3.30.

COUNTRY	LOSSES
UK	51 confirmed dead 416 missing presumed dead 701 individuals whose whereabouts are not confirmed
Germany	784 dead or presumed dead 250 unaccounted for
Sweden	689 confirmed or presumed dead 1200 unaccounted for

Figure 3.30 Some provisional figures for casualties among travellers

Impacts on countries in the region

We shall now look at some of the impacts created by this extreme natural event, and we begin with a consideration of the disaster's immediate effects on tourism in Thailand.

Thailand

The Gulf of Thailand was unaffected by the disaster and all resorts located in this part of the country (Ko Samui, Hua Hin, Ko Pha Ngan, Pattaya and Ko Samet) remained open for business as usual. It was the areas of the west coast that took the full force of the giant wave, particularly Phuket, Krabi and Khao Lak (see Figure 3.31). The island of Phuket, the most popular resort on the coast, was the scene of some of the worst damage and loss of life. Twenty-four hotels were destroyed or severely damaged. A further 29 were still able to operate,

Figure 3.31 An example of the damage caused by the tsunami

but had sustained damage ranging from flooding and destruction of some rooms to loss of water and power.

Patong and Kamala were both particularly badly hit, with the large Merlin resort completely destroyed and the Holiday Inn and Amari Coral Beach badly damaged.

Khao Lak was devastated by the disaster, with most properties damaged beyond repair and hundreds of fatalities. On Ko Phi Phi, a favoured destination for backpackers, much of the accommodation was in budget beach huts, many of which were completely destroyed. At Krabi, resorts on high ground were unaffected, but there was destruction at beach level, where Rayavadee and the Krabi Resort Hotel were badly hit.

It has been estimated that Thailand's tourist island of Phuket lost US$10 million a day during the early new-year peak season in the wake of the tsunami. Beaches normally packed with tourists escaping the northern hemisphere's winter were practically deserted, and Phuket had just a 20 per cent hotel occupancy rate. The numbers were bound to remain low, especially in terms of European travellers from countries that suffered hundreds or even thousands of casualties from the waves.

Tourism accounts for some 6 per cent of Thailand's gross domestic product. Phuket alone generates 72 billion baht in tourism revenue each year. During the peak Christmas and new-year period, revenues can be expected to double and so the destination actually lost about 400 million baht per day. Most of the visitors to the destination in the immediate aftermath were rescue and relief workers, outside volunteers, and hundreds of diplomatic staff and forensic personnel tending to the needs of the thousands of foreign tourists who were on Phuket at the time of the disaster.

The heavy financial losses were expected to last through to March 2005, until many of the affected properties could be rebuild enough to reopen. However, the damage in the eyes of the international community may take many more months to repair. Many of the most dramatic video images of the waves crashing into resorts and towns were taken by tourists on Phuket's west coast. Local authorities quickly began a campaign to assure foreign governments and travel agencies that Phuket will bounce back quickly. However, nearly 20 000 people lost their jobs, and the government has promised to find jobs for displaced workers and offer relief measures to businesses.

We will now briefly explore the tsunami's effects on other destinations in the region.

Malaysia

Resort areas around Penang were most affected. No hotels were reported to have closed, although water damage and debris were widespread. On Langkawi, the Pelangi Beach resort was badly damaged and Berjaya resort also suffered damage to its beach area.

The Maldives

Some islands suffered severe damage but many areas were sheltered from the destructive force of the main wave. The tourist board estimated that out of 87 resorts only 19 had to be closed, due to varying degrees of damage. Within the destination as a whole, major hotels that were forced to close included Soneva Gili, The Four Seasons, Taj Exotica and Velavaru.

Sri Lanka

Just over half of Sri Lanka's 14 000 rooms were affected. Sri Lanka Tourism estimated that 48 large properties, mainly in southern resorts such as Bentota and Galle, suffered damage and almost half of these had to be closed. Among those damaged beyond repair was the Yala Safari Game Lodge.

India

The coast of Tamil Nadu was devastated and there were many casualties. In the town and temple site of Mahabalipuram, a popular attraction for Western tourists, fifteen people were reported dead and surrounding resorts were damaged.

Indonesia

Tourist centres such as Bali and Lombok were unaffected. The worst-hit areas were in Aceh, northwest Sumatra – about which the UK Foreign Office had already established a longstanding warning against non-essential travel due to civil unrest. The Foreign Office reinforced its warning in the light of the earthquake disaster.

The Seychelles

Three thousand miles from the earthquake's epicentre, the Seychelles were spared the worst effects of the tsunami. Three hotels located on Praslin were temporarily closed: the Paradise Sun, La Reserve I and Vacanze Cote d'Or Lodge. Other hotels with some flood damage included Cafés des Arts and Palm Beach.

East Africa

Kenya experienced unusually high swells, with slight damage in Mombasa, but all resorts were reported to be operating normally. Travel industry sources reported that tourist areas in Tanzania were also unaffected.

Possible effects on world tourism

The number of victims claimed by this unprecedented natural disaster, among both the local populations and the visitors in their midst, has been described as the highest in history. An immediate reaction is to ask to what extent it has affected world tourism, a source of economic activity and cultural enrichment for the countries concerned – as indeed for most other countries of the world. Taking world tourism as a whole, the answer has to be that the impact will be slight, for the following reasons.

Although the five most severely affected destinations – India, Indonesia, The Maldives, Thailand and Sri Lanka – are making tremendous strides in their tourism development and having considerable success as tourist destinations, they achieved a market share of only 3 per cent of total world tourist arrivals in 2004. In the other Asian countries hit by the tsunami, especially Malaysia, the affected areas are either not highly developed tourist destinations or are already recovering.

In 2004 this region of the world enjoyed the greatest expansion of both its economy and its tourism. South-east Asia's growth rate outstripped that of the region as a whole in a year marked by a vigorous recovery from the sharp downturn in growth caused by the SARS outbreak and the unstable climate of 2003. Asia made spectacular economic advances in 2004, as reflected in the results of many countries of the region and of the main generators of tourism in particular. It is estimated that, in 2004, gross domestic products (GDPs) rose by the following amounts:

* Australia – 3.6 per cent

* Japan – 4.4 per cent

* India – 6.4 per cent

* Republic of Korea – 8.8 per cent

* China – 9.0 per cent.

This has boosted every kind of tourism, especially that *within* the region which accounts for 79 per cent of the region's total arrivals. Furthermore, the human catastrophe and the material losses caused by the tsunami have been confined to a few coastal resorts in each country, and the damage in some cases is quite limited.

All in all, it can be assumed that the volume of tourism actually affected in the five countries in question will account for less than one per cent of total world arrivals. There are therefore solid grounds for hoping that a prompt recovery of those destinations will pave the way for co-operation and that tourism will help to mitigate the devastating effects on the local population.

The perception the tourist has of the disaster is that it was a freak and distressing event wholly unprecedented in the Indian Ocean. The disaster has brought tragedy to the local population and hit tourism hard. There is, however, a great divide between the perception people have of the event, owing to the considerable coverage given to it by the media – an example of the globalization phenomenon – and the expected consequences for the development of world tourism. Although there was great hardship initially, tourism is expected to recover in the short term and be only slightly affected during 2005.

Knowledge check

1 *To help you appreciate the varied nature of destinations and to understand the key factors in their development.*

Choose a destination and examine how it has changed through time (at least for the last 10 years or so) in terms of:

- new building developments
- numbers of visitors (day visits, overnight visits and overseas visitors)
- new events
- new attractions
- variety of locations within the destination and their uses
- the agents of tourism development and the roles of the private, public and voluntary sectors
- support facilities in place.

2 *To help you understand the ways in which particular locations appeal to particular types of tourist and visitor.*

Find an example of each of the following and obtain an image and description of each location:

- beach resort
- countryside area
- historical destination
- ski resort
- inclusive holiday centre
- conference/major event venue.

Using only the image, describe the reasons certain groups of tourist might be attracted to it.

3 *To help you to appreciate the major factors influencing destination appeal.*

For the six destinations previously researched and identified, provide full details of the following:

- location (landscape features)
- climate
- accessibility (internal and external)
- accommodation
- attractions (natural and built)
- culture (dress, arts and crafts, performance, language and religion).

Resources

The following long- and short-haul destinations currently actively promote themselves to the travel trade and encourage agency staff to take advantage of specialised destination training:

✱ Malta Tourist Office – www.maltawiz.com

✱ Singapore Tourism Board – www.singa-pro.co.uk

✱ Hong Kong Tourism Board – www.discoverhongkong.com

✱ South African Tourism – www.southafrica.net

✱ Caribbean Tourism Organisation – www.caribbean.co.uk

✱ Jamaica Tourist Board – www.visitjamaica.com

✱ Tourism Authority of Thailand – www.training.thaismile.co.uk

✱ Tourism Ireland – www.irelandexpert.co.uk

✱ Kiwi Specialist Programme – www.newzealand.com/travel/trade

✱ Spanish Tourist Office – www.tourspain.co.uk

✱ Jordan Tourism Board – www.jordanambassador.com

✱ Tourism Australia – www.specialist.australia.com

✱ Jersey Tourism – www.jersey.com/trade

✱ Dubai DTCM – www.dubaitourism.ae

✱ Seychelles SMART – www.aspureasitgets.com

✱ Bermuda Tourism – www.bermudatourism.com

✱ LA Travel Academy – www.seemyLA.com

✱ Bahamas Tourist Office – www.bahamacademy.co.uk

✱ Visit USA Association – www.visitusa.org.uk

✱ Canadian Tourism Commission – www.canada-counsellors.co.uk

You may also find the following websites to be of use:

✱ www.about.com

✱ www.tourist-offices.org.uk

* www.whatsonwhen.com
* www.musee-online.org
* www.unmissable.com
* www.worldclimate.com
* www.tripprep.com
* www.fco.gov.uk/travel
* www.viamichelin.com
* www.oanda.com/convert/cheatsheet
* www.travelknowledge.com
* www.americanexpress.com
* www.staruk.org.uk
* www.towd.com
* www.travelchannel.co.uk

Newspaper articles will often be stored on the paper's website and these are an excellent source of additional information. For example, if specific information were required about tourism developments in Dubai or the wider UAE, then items in the local press could be investigated at www.gulf-news.com from an on-line edition by selecting 'Search' from the footer bar. Similar arrangements will exist for other publications. Finally, the search process will reveal many other sources of appropriate information. It is well worth looking at some specialist geography sites as they frequently contain excellent travel and tourism material. In particular, www.geoprojects.co.uk and www.geographyonline.co.uk has further interesting resource material.

Glossary

Casual staff
Casual staff are those employed from time to time to deal with work peaks.

Complaints procedures
Complaints procedures are usually made known to the customer, so that the customer understands the types of processes to be followed and the structure for expressing dissatisfaction.

Direct employment
Direct employment is jobs that are in hotels, tourist accommodation, travel agencies, tour operators, tourist attractions etc.

Disability Discrimination Act 1995
In terms of the Act, disability means a physical or mental impairment that has a substantial and long-term adverse effect on a person's ability to carry out normal day-to-day activities.

External customers
External customers are those we normally consider to be 'the customers', and these are the people who buy the products or services of the organisation and come from outside the organisation itself.

Fly/drive
Hiring a car as a pre-paid part of a holiday package is known as a fly/drive holiday. The car is frequently picked up at the airport at the destination.

Focus group
The composition of a focus group may vary according to the organisation, but it is often a cross-section of employees and users. The aim is to focus discussion on a specific area of the organisation, or a specific problem

Gross national product
The gross national product (GNP) is the measure of a country's total economic production, calculated by adding the value of all goods and services produced to the net revenue from abroad.

Housekeeping
Housekeeping means that the guests' rooms are cleaned, beds made and towels changed.

Inclusive tour
An inclusive tour is another name for a package holiday.

Independent tour
Independent tours are any form of travel that is not part of a package holiday, when travellers put their own itinerary together.

Indirect employment
Indirect employment is in, for example, the decor of a hotel, the printer supplying the brochures for a tour operator, and the web designer of the website for an airline.

Integration
Integration is the combination of two or more companies under the same control for mutual benefit.

Internal customers
Internal customers are other employees within the organisation. They might be colleagues with whom you work closely, or other employees in a different department or in other branches. They might be regular suppliers of goods and services who deal with the organisation perhaps on a contract basis.

Legislation
Legislation consists principally of Acts of Parliament passed by central government. Local authorities can introduce by-laws that apply only locally.

Long-haul destination
From the UK, long-haul destinations are those beyond Europe, such as Australia, the Far East, the USA and India.

Overseas visitor
An overseas visitor is a person who, being permanently resident in a country outside the UK, visits the UK for a period of less than 12 months. UK citizens resident overseas for 12 months or more coming home on leave are included in this category.

Principals
Principals is the name given to companies that a travel agent does business with, commonly tour operators, airlines, ferry , rail and car hire companies and hotel groups.

Product knowledge

The more you know about the product or service you are selling, the better advice and guidance you can give to customers. This is called product knowledge.

Public image

Public image is the perception customers have of an organisation.

Seasonal staff

Seasonal staff are those employed only during the main season.

Seasonality

Tourism demand regularly fluctuates over the course of a year. This is known as seasonality.

Short break

Many domestic tourists in the UK now favour the short break. This is usually a weekend or mid-week break of three nights or less.

Short-haul destination

From the UK, short-haul destinations are usually in continental Europe, under four hours' flight time away from the UK.

Stakeholder

A stakeholder is an interested party in a non-commercial organisation, such as a member of a charity or a taxpayer.

Tourism promotion

Tourism promotion is the name given to the business of persuading tourists to visit a particular area.

Value for money

Value for money is a concept that is difficult to describe, and it is something that individuals will define differently. One might ask 'Does the park offer us more for our money at a better quality?' Another might ask 'If our family spends a day there, will there be enough for us to do and enjoy to make the initial expense worth while?' Each is asking about value for money in different terms.

Viewdata

Viewdata consisted of a screen that displayed information transmitted by phone lines. In 1987, 85 per cent of all package holidays were booked through this system.

Visitor attraction

A visitor (or tourist) attraction can be defined as a permanently established excursion destination, a primary purpose of which is to allow public access for entertainment, interest or education, rather than being a primary retail outlet or venue for sporting, theatrical or film performances. It must be open to the public, without prior booking, for published periods each year, and should be capable of attracting day visitors or tourists as well as local residents.

Index

Page numbers in *italics* refer to illustrations, those in **bold** refer to definitions.

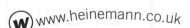